"Being a digital immigrant, *Gen Z in Work* was nothing short of provocative and intellectually stimulating theatre that helped grasp the rich tapestry of these Gen Z digital natives. Self-defeating loops such as 'The Job Crises Loop' are common patterns in an organizational malfunction that every leader would do well to know."

Prof. Dr. Barkev Kassarjian, *Professor Emeritus of Strategy and Organization, The International Institute for Management Development (IMD), Switzerland, Professor Emeritus of Management, Babson College, USA, Former Professor of Organizational Behavior at Harvard Business School, USA*

"Ochis's book could not be more timely, insightful, and thought-provoking. As a corporate and civil society leader managing multi-generational teams, this book has made me think afresh. It provides research, scholarship, and advice which practitioners would find invaluable in supporting the performance and development of their teams and improving organizational effectiveness."

Lucian J. Hudson, *Professor-in-Practice in Leadership & Organizations, Durham University Business School, UK*

"At a time when corporate environments are transformed by AI, social revolutions, and rapid technological innovations, Karina Ochis provides innovative solutions to creating a workplace that embraces an age-diverse office population."

Prof. Dr. Asher Orkaby, *Harvard University, USA*

"*Gen Z in Work* offers strategies for employers to better understand and engage with Gen Z employees, ultimately leading to more prosperous and productive work environments. I strongly recommend this book to all types of organizations who seek to understand and effectively engage with the youngest generation in the workforce."

Prof. Dr. M. Amr Sadik, *Board Member and Professor of HR Management at GUST, Latvia HR & Strategy Management Adjunct Professor from IPE Management School, Paris*

"Employee engagement is at the heart of what ensures a good strategy becomes unbeatable! Going through the book, I discovered binding opportunities, realized where – and why – mistakes were made, and uncovered inconsistencies that demotivated. My discoveries were not limited to Gen Z, which shows the power of the frameworks that Karina has built. This book is a deep analysis of Organizational Leadership."

Prof. Dr. Joe Pons, *President of AXIOMA Marketing Consultants, Spain, IESE International Graduate School of Management, Spain, Instituto Internacional San Telmo in Seville, Spain, Visiting Professor at the IEDC – Bled School of Management, Slovenia*

GEN Z IN WORK

This concise and clear book provides actionable solutions to every manager's and leader's newest problem: How to work effectively with Gen Z employees.

Employee disengagement is a problem for businesses around the globe, with 85% of employees actively disengaged from their work. By 2025, Gen Z will account for one-third of the workforce, according to the World Economic Forum, and a growing challenge is how to adapt organizations to effectively include this group. Companies must now redesign long-established practices to include rapid integration, gamified rewards, mixed generation teams, and multigeneration training in ways that will capitalize on the current behaviors of Gen Z, as well as other worker groups.

This book provides:

- The measures companies can take to forge productive relationships between Gen Z and older, more experienced employees.
- An approach that can be readily applied by senior executives and managers to engage Gen Z employees and to address the disengagement problem more broadly.
- Implementable solutions on how five traditional practices – onboarding, leadership, culture, motivation, and benefits – can be altered in companies to improve Gen Z productivity.

The problem of disengagement is widespread across companies and industries and results in diminished productivity, high turnover costs, and the loss of experienced professionals. Managers and leaders across all sectors will find this book indispensable in implementing an actionable strategy for improving the performance of Gen Z.

Karina Ochis is Professor of Leadership and Management, as well as an author, speaker, and executive consultant. She is a global expert in leading the four generations of employees. An accomplished public speaker, Karina participates at worldwide conferences and summits including TEDx and has been featured in *Entrepreneur*, *Forbes*, and *The Huffington Post*.

GEN Z IN WORK

A PRACTICAL GUIDE TO ENGAGING EMPLOYEES ACROSS THE GENERATIONS

Karina Ochis

Routledge
Taylor & Francis Group

LONDON AND NEW YORK

Designed cover image: Getty Images

First published 2025
by Routledge
4 Park Square, Milton Park, Abingdon, Oxon OX14 4RN

and by Routledge
605 Third Avenue, New York, NY 10158

Routledge is an imprint of the Taylor & Francis Group, an informa business

© 2025 Karina Ochis

British Library Cataloguing-in-Publication Data
A catalogue record for this book is available from the British Library

Library of Congress Cataloging-in-Publication Data
Names: Ochis, Karina, author.
Title: Gen Z in work: a practical guide to engaging employees across the generations / Karina Ochis.
Other titles: Generation Z in work
Description: Abingdon, Oxon; New York, NY: Routledge, 2025. |
Includes bibliographical references and index.
Subjects: LCSH: Generation Z—Employment. | Generation Z—Attitudes. |
Conflict of generations in the workplace.
Classification: LCC HF5549.5.C75 O24 2025 (print) | LCC HF5549.5.C75 (ebook) |
DDC 658.30084/2—dc23/eng/20240927
LC record available at https://lccn.loc.gov/2024033865
LC ebook record available at https://lccn.loc.gov/2024033866

ISBN: 978-1-032-72250-4 (hbk)
ISBN: 978-1-032-69309-5 (pbk)
ISBN: 978-1-032-72269-6 (ebk)

DOI: 10.4324/9781032722696

Typeset in Bembo
by codeMantra

To the future generations of leaders: May you become who you were meant to be, fulfill your true potential, live to serve humanity, and turn out to be the change agents we know you are!

CONTENTS

FOREWORD

Navigate the complexities of today's multigenerational workforce with authority and ease. *Gen Z in Work*, by the esteemed Professor Dr. Karina Ochis, provides an indispensable roadmap for harnessing the unique strengths of Boomers to Gen Z, ensuring your leadership legacy is as dynamic as the teams you manage.

Dr. Karina Ochis is a distinguished leader and researcher in workplace dynamics. As the foremost authority in the multigenerational leadership field, her work blends extensive academic research with practical, real-world applications, providing profound insights into the complexities and nuances of today's increasingly diverse workforce, which spans multiple generations.

Dr. Ochis has worked countless hours on this practitioner guidebook with different generations at various management levels to help them navigate the challenges and opportunities arising from workforce collaboration. *Gen Z in work* positions all-encompassing arguments and observations based on years of extensive research and lived experience. Moreover, Dr. Ochis' expertise in the subject matter pertains brilliantly to academic research and real-world practice.

Gen Z in Work outlines how diverse ages characterize the present-day workplace, each bringing unique perspectives and skills. This diversity, while beneficial, presents specific challenges and opportunities that require nuanced understanding and management. Acknowledging distinctions in communication style, work preferences, and technological proficiency among the generations is essential. Dr. Ochis does not merely analyze these dynamics; she offers a meticulously crafted guidebook filled with actionable steps and key takeaways. These strategies, designed to be immediately implemented, empower you to enhance collaboration and foster an inclusive environment where every generation can thrive.

Professor Ochis delves deep into the generational divides that can lead to conflict and misunderstanding within the workplace. With her expertise in generational theory, she aids managers and employees alike in fostering better relationships across generational lines. *Gen Z in Work* articulately presents the distinct values, beliefs, working styles, and behaviors that characterize each generation, emphasizing the unique strengths and competencies they bring. *Gen Z in Work* focuses on creating diverse, inclusive, equitable, and collaborative workplaces.

The insights from *Gen Z in Work* are transformative. They promise intergenerational cooperation, improved productivity, enhanced communication, and greater employee satisfaction. These elements are crucial for any organization aiming to foster personal and professional growth among its staff.

Professor Dr. Karina Ochis is recognized as a pioneer in addressing multigenerational challenges within diverse industries worldwide. This book is an academic treatise and a practical manual encouraging generational understanding, cooperation, and collaboration. It highlights the critical roles of mentorship and reverse mentorship in facilitating knowledge and skill transfer across different age groups, enhancing professional development, and cultivating a culture of mutual respect and knowledge-sharing. Through training, teaching, and knowledge-sharing, organizations can cultivate an environment where each generation feels appreciated and can work in a more harmonious working atmosphere.

This book is a significant contribution to the field, an indispensable resource, and a must-have for anyone managing or working within a multigenerational workforce. Professor Ochis' dedication and passion for her subject matter shine through in this seminal work, ensuring her legacy will continue influencing future generations of workers and leaders.

– Professor Dr. Oxford York, PhD, CCC, CAGCS, CCTP,
Human Factors Scientific Research Specialist / Advanced Clinical
Trauma and Grief Counseling Specialist, Canada

PREFACE

In the annals of management and leadership, a seismic shift is unfolding with the rise of Generation Z (Gen Z) – the youngest generational group to enter the workforce. This youngest and digitally adept cohort is not just joining the ranks; they are reimagining them, bringing a distinct set of values and expectations, and reshaping the traditional workplace. In an era where the blend of generational diversity is more the rule than the exception, the imperative to understand and engage effectively with employees across different age groups has reached an unprecedented level. The stakes are high: intergenerational friction can lead to disengagement, and disengagement can be costly regarding turnover and the broader financial impact on organizations.

Gen Z in Work: A Practical Guide to Engaging Employees Across the Generations is a roadmap for navigating this new terrain, where understanding each generation is not just beneficial but essential for the success and sustainability of organizations in a rapidly evolving world. As we delve into the book's pages, we are presented with unique insights gleaned from rigorous research and actionable solutions.

The genesis of this book is rooted in a decade-long journey across four continents, during which I sought to bridge the generational divide as a leadership professor and consultant. Through extensive research, including speeches, workshops, and consulting with business leaders, a profound need was identified: to address the generational clash and equip emerging workers with essential skills and wisdom. This book arises from practical, real-world challenges, aiming to illuminate the path toward generational harmony and understanding.

Allow me to unveil the tapestry of this book's creation. Global leaders admitted that when it came to young recruits, they were peering into the abyss. Each one grappled with a profound conundrum: how to forge the leadership pathways of the future and how to equip the emerging generations of workers with the tools and skills they sorely lacked. Meanwhile, young generations of employees roamed the world of work without the guiding hand of mentors. It became abundantly clear that a seismic clash between generations was unfolding before our eyes, fraught with tension and seemingly irreconcilable differences. The lament of the times echoed loudly – a cry for resolution in a landscape characterized by uncertainty.

A troubling reality is at the heart of today's corporate world: widespread employee disengagement. Tenured employees might react by wagering war on Gen Z troops, attempting to mold them into a preconceived corporate mold. Yet such a strategy perpetuates intergenerational strife and exacerbates the very disengagement we aim to conquer. This book challenges conventional approaches, advocating for a reimagined alignment with Gen Z's nuances instead of forcing them into traditional frameworks.

Gen Z in Work provides a comprehensive view of Gen Z in the workplace, covering their traits, expectations, values, and lifecycle. We are also confronted with exploring the three primary forces propelling Gen Z disengagement – a trifecta of unrealistic expectations, generational friction, and the power imbalances that permeate our organizations. It transcends industry boundaries, offering universal insights for leaders and managers in diverse fields. This guide diagnoses the challenges of multigenerational management and presents remedies, including strategies for addressing disengagement trends, enhancing productivity, and fostering multigenerational collaboration.

Readers are equipped with the knowledge and tools to effectively engage the youngest generation in the workforce, bridging gaps and fostering a collaborative, productive environment. This guide is a key to unlocking the potential of a luminous, engaged future in the modern, multigenerational workplace.

Nevertheless, let *Gen Z in Work* be more than just a guide; let it be a catalyst for change in your professional world. This book is my ode to the future of work – a future that demands understanding and tolerance and a wholehearted embrace of the diverse generational talents that populate our offices. Together, we can unlock the potential of a vibrant, engaged, and harmonious multigenerational workplace. This is not just my vision; it is a shared future we can all look forward to with optimism and excitement. Join me in turning the page on outdated workplace dynamics and writing a new chapter on inclusive, dynamic, and effective intergenerational collaboration.

ACKNOWLEDGMENTS

Firstly, I would like to thank my professors and mentors from the UK to Italy, Switzerland, and the US for their diligence and insightfulness, commentary, and professional guidance on leadership, engagement, and generational theories.

Second, I acknowledge executive clients from over the four continents with whom I consulted, the leaders and practicing managers who formed the audiences at my speaking and training events, and doctoral candidates whose sharing of intergenerational challenges has been pivotal in fulfilling this work.

Lastly, I would like to acknowledge and thank the many professionals, both Gen Z and managers of Gen Z, who were interviewed and shaped the research. The interest of both younger and older generational groups in better understanding the problem of generations in the workplace has provided me with abundant insights and reassurance in performing research in this understudied domain. Their encouragement and knowledge are appreciated and have been instrumental to the successful completion of the book.

ACRONYMS AND ABBREVIATIONS

AI	Artificial Intelligence
CIO	Chief Information Officer
EVLN	Exit, Voice, Loyalty, Neglect Model
GEN	Generation
HRM	Human Resource Management
IS	Information System
TMT	Top Management Team

GLOSSARY

Generation   A generation is fabricated by society and encompasses an array of factors, including age, defining historical events, trends, and their understanding (Mannheim, 1952).

Generational Cohort / Group   Demographic unit (Ryder, 1965); a proxy measure for traits, dispositions, and behaviors and the social relationships in which they are embedded, created to provide theoretically meaningful interpretation (Hardy & Waite, 1997).

Multigenerational Workforce   A workforce comprises employees of more than one generational group (Dwyer & Azevedo, 2016).

Intergenerational Conflict   The identity-based conflict between generations is based on perceived similarities and differences in work values, psychological traits, career patterns, motivation, learning orientation, commitment and retention, leadership styles and preferences, and levels of creativity (Urick et al., 2017).

The Millennial Problem   This is a set of ideas according to which Generation Y individuals, the second youngest generation, also known as Millennials, are ill-fit for the work environment and represent a problem (Lancaster & Stillman, 2003).

Generation Z   Individuals born after 1996 who are now penetrating the workforce (Dimock, 2019).

Generation Y   Millennials, also known as Generation Y, are the demographic cohort following Generation X and preceding Generation Z. This group includes individuals born from the early 1980s to the mid-1990s to the early 2000s. Millennials are known for their comfort with communication technology, media, and digital environments as they came of age during the rise of the internet, social media, and mobile technology (Twenge, 2010).

Generation X   "Generation X" refers to the demographic cohort following the Baby Boomers and preceding the Millennials. Generally, this generation includes individuals born from the mid-1960s to the early 1980s. Generation X is characterized by its experience of significant social, economic, and technological changes (Twenge, 2010).

Boomers   "Boomers," or "Baby Boomers," refer to the generational cohort born approximately between 1946 and 1964. This generation emerged following World War II during a period marked by a significant increase in birth rates, hence the term "baby boom" (Fry, 2019).

Engagement   The process of encouraging people to be interested in the work of an organization is the fact of being involved with something (Cambridge Dictionary, 2024).

Leader   A person who leads a group of people, especially the head of an organization (Oxford English Dictionary, 2024).

Leadership   Position of a leader; ability to lead; the position of a group of people leading or influencing others within a given context; the group itself; the action or influence necessary for the direction or organization of effort in a group undertaking (Oxford English Dictionary, 2024).

Follower   A person who decides whether or not to collaborate with a leader to achieve an organizational purpose (Kelley, 1988).

Management   Organization, supervision, or direction is the application of skill or care in the manipulation, use, treatment, or control of the conduct of something (Oxford English Dictionary, 2024).

Multigenerational Leadership   It entails the consideration of a multitude of elements in the process of leadership, ranging from leadership preferences to work values and characteristics of various generational cohorts (Dwyer & Azenvedo, 2016).

Power   One's potential or capacity to influence others through various means (French & Raven, 1959).

NOTE ON TERMINOLOGY

The terms "leaders," "employees," and "individuals" are used extensively. It is essential to understand that these terms are intended to be inclusive of all gender identities. The references to "Generation X, Y, Z" and "Boomers" also encompass individuals of all genders within these generational groups.

PART I

CORE CONCEPTS – UNDERSTANDING THE GENERATIONAL LANDSCAPE

INTRODUCTION

Abstract

This first chapter sets the stage for *Gen Z in Work*, introducing the profound shift in today's corporate landscape. Highlighting the widespread issue of employee disengagement, the chapter lays the groundwork for understanding the complexities and nuances of managing a multigenerational workforce. It elaborates on the urgency for companies to adapt swiftly to the multifaceted dynamics introduced by Gen Z to avoid further disengagement and alienation among the workforce. Moreover, this chapter extends beyond Gen Z, acknowledging the diversity within the workforce and the importance of harmonizing the needs of all generational cohorts. It proposes a strategic approach to multigenerational leadership tailored to meet the distinct requirements of Gen Z while fostering an inclusive environment for all age groups.

Welcome to the battleground of today's corporate frontier, where the arrival of Generation Z (Gen Z) in the workforce is rewriting the rules of engagement. According to the State of the Global Workplace report, a concerning 85% of employees have been disengaged at work, leading to an estimated $7 trillion in global productivity losses (Harter, 2017). However, employee engagement has seen a resurgence, reaching a record high of 23% in 2023 (Gallup Inc, 2023). This fluctuation in engagement levels has had significant economic implications, costing the global economy of $8.8 trillion or 9% of global GDP (Gallup Inc, 2023).

DOI: 10.4324/9781032722696-2

This is not another generational shift but a revolution in the making. Generation Z, the latest entrants in the workforce, stands distinct in their engagement with work, showing alarming signs of stress and burnout (Pendell & Vander Helm, 2022). This generation has sparked a significant trend, 'quiet quitting,' where over half of the global workforce engages in minimal effort, performing only core tasks without further psychological involvement (Klotz & Bolino, 2022; McGregor, 2022; Smith, 2022). This phenomenon, indicative of a broader disengagement crisis (Johnson, 2023), prompts a reassessment of traditional management approaches, especially as managers often show a preference for working with older generations (Munnell et al., 2006; Pitt-Catsouphes et al., 2007).

THE COST OF DISENGAGEMENT: A GENERATIONAL CHALLENGE

Research shows that age-related preferences strongly influence employee engagement in the workplace (James et al., 2011). Today's leaders face the daunting task of aligning these diverse generational needs within their organizations while avoiding potential conflicts. Millennials and Gen Z often struggle to assimilate within traditional corporate structures (Ruggeri, 2017), underscoring the need for a nuanced approach to multigenerational leadership.

The rising disengagement among Gen Z employees is not just a workplace anomaly; it represents a significant financial burden in terms of lost productivity and turnover. Traditional motivational strategies and complex integration schemes have failed to address this challenge. This book posits a critical argument: the lack of power-sharing in the employer-employee relationship leads to Gen Z's withdrawal, either mentally or through actual resignation. As their sentiments echo, "What else can we do?"

TRANSFORMING THE WORKPLACE

Today's central question for leaders is how to engage Generation Z actively within a diverse workforce. This book argues for a proactive approach to understanding and integrating Gen Z, as their participation is crucial for organizations' longevity and future success.

Gen Z in Work aims to be an essential field guide to understanding and harnessing this new cohort's unique dynamics. As over half of the global workforce teeters on the brink of disengagement, with 'quiet quitting' – whether perceived as a novel or old-time concept – becoming the new norm (McGregor, 2022; Smith, 2022), this book offers a radical approach to reinvigorating the workplace and aligning it with the aspirations of the most digitally fluent generation to date.

Discover how to transform these challenges into opportunities and lead organizations into a new era of productivity and engagement. Companies' specific response to Gen Z disruptors depends on managers' ability to execute quickly. The longer managers wait to adapt to the multigenerational phenomenon, the more companies risk alienating young recruits and fostering further disengagement between the generational groups at work.

CRACKING THE GEN Z CODE: A STRATEGIC GUIDE FOR MULTIGENERATIONAL ENGAGEMENT

Gen Z in Work offers more than just insights into this newest workforce cohort; it provides a comprehensive toolkit designed to excel in the Gen Z era. This resource guides readers through the nuanced landscape of Gen Z's workplace expectations, their preferred leadership styles, and their aspirations for work-life balance. Key areas such as onboarding, leadership, organizational culture, motivation, and benefits are thoroughly explored to empower leaders in tailoring their strategies to Gen Z's distinctive needs. This approach enhances Gen Z engagement and strengthens intergenerational relationships within teams, addressing the broader issue of employee disengagement.

SCOPE AND LIMITATIONS OF THE BOOK: BEYOND GENERATIONAL COHORTS

The scope of this book extends beyond Gen Z. It acknowledges that while Gen Z may be the disruptors in the workplace, the narrative of a successful organization involves understanding and harmonizing the diverse needs and values of all generational cohorts. This book delves into building influential intergenerational groups, fostering a culture of engagement and collaborative synergy across all ages.

Additionally, this resource emphasizes the importance of embracing all generational groups and advocating for creating collaborative and diverse teams that leverage the strengths of every generation in the modern business landscape.

While framed within the context of generational cohorts, the insights and strategies presented equally apply to diverse age groups, transcending rigid generational labels. This book focuses primarily on generational dynamics but recognizes that not every individual ascribes strictly to their generational cohort's typical characteristics based on several factors, including background, ethnicity, culture, education level, and others that are the subject of academic debate and will not be treated here.

Importantly, this book does not delve deeply into the complexities of gender identity, expression, and the diverse spectrum of gender experiences. The references to gender within this publication are intended to contribute to the broader understanding of workplace dynamics. They are not meant to define or limit the experiences and identities of individuals. As such, the book and the research purposely do not ascribe to a gender split.

This book does not delve into macroeconomic factors or global economic policies indirectly influencing workforce trends. Instead, it concentrates on universal principles applicable across various business contexts rather than industry-specific challenges. While it touches upon technological advancements like artificial intelligence (AI), this book does not provide a detailed analysis of these technologies or their specific impacts on employment practices. Its core focus is on interpersonal dynamics, leadership strategies, and organizational culture tailored to Generation Z and adaptable to broader age groups within the workforce.

By maintaining this focus, *Gen Z in Work* aims to offer targeted, actionable insights for managers and leaders. It provides tools for understanding and managing a workforce that, while often segmented into generational cohorts, is more accurately represented by a spectrum of individual experiences and perspectives. This approach underscores the book's relevance in addressing the immediate and practical aspects of fostering an engaging, inclusive, and productive workplace environment for all employees, regardless of their generational affiliation.

WHO WILL BENEFIT FROM THIS BOOK?

Primarily aimed at managers and leaders in various sectors, this book is an essential guide for navigating the challenges a multigenerational workforce poses. Its insights are relevant to professionals at all career stages, making it an asset for middle managers, senior leaders, consultants, and recent graduates. Institutional buyers and academic institutions will also find this book beneficial as it addresses the universal challenge of employee disengagement and offers practical solutions.

Gen Z readers will find this book especially enlightening, offering a mirror to their workplace experiences and expectations. It provides an opportunity to understand the dynamics of their generation and learn how to navigate the multigenerational corporate landscape effectively. This book is a roadmap for Gen Z employees to harness their strengths and thrive in the workplace, fostering mutual understanding and collaboration across all generations.

NAVIGATING THE BOOK: A STRATEGIC APPROACH

Classifying the table of contents into three parts with subsequent chapters is meticulously designed to provide a logical progression for understanding and managing a multigenerational workforce. **Part I: Core Concepts – Understanding the Generational Landscape** establishes a foundational understanding of the diverse generational dynamics within the workplace, which is essential for leaders to appreciate the broader context. Moving into **Part II: Hands-On Leadership – Actionable Strategies for Gen Z Integration**, the focus shifts to practical, actionable strategies explicitly tailored to harness the potential of Generation Z. This section equips leaders with the tools needed to engage this new cohort actively. Lastly, **Part III: Toolkit for Transformation – Short Guides for Implementation** offers concise, targeted guides for quick implementation, allowing leaders to apply insights and strategies immediately.

Readers are advised to adopt a systematic approach to benefit from this book. This structured approach enhances comprehension and facilitates the practical application of knowledge across different layers of organizational leadership. Begin with an understanding of the generational profiles of Baby Boomers, Generation X, Millennials, and Generation Z, detailed in Chapters 4 and 5, forming the foundation for comprehending intergenerational dynamics. However, each chapter also offers stand-alone value, allowing readers to focus on areas of immediate interest. Engage actively with the content, apply the "Eight Actions You Can Take Today" in Chapter 19, and use this book to reflect and improve in managing a diverse, dynamic workforce.

A CHAPTER-BY-CHAPTER BREAKDOWN: SUMMARIES

Part I: Core Concepts – Understanding the Generational Landscape

Chapter 1: Introduction – The Genesis of the Multigenerational Challenge

The opening chapter introduces business leaders' critical challenges in today's workforce, particularly regarding Generation Z's unique disengagement. This chapter sets the stage for a comprehensive examination of Gen Z's impact on the workplace, outlining the book's objectives and the insights that await the reader.

Chapter 2: Welcome to the Modern Workforce – Understanding the New Employment Landscape

This chapter examines the current state of the global workforce, helping readers answer the perennial question: What is happening in the world of work? Readers will explore burgeoning workplace trends, including artificial intelligence, that describe the multigenerational workplace. They will equip themselves with the knowledge and language needed to navigate the complexities of today's diverse workforce.

Chapter 3: Are You a Multigenerational Manager? – A Reflective Analysis

Central to this analysis is the grappling with a critical question: What defines a multigenerational leader? This chapter delves into the essence of this leadership style, underscoring that it is not just about recognizing the distinct preferences of different age groups. Instead, the secret to successful multigenerational leadership lies in mastering the dynamics of collaboration among diverse generational groups.

Chapter 4: What Is a Generation at Work? – Defining Generations

This chapter explores the concept of generations. It clarifies prevailing concepts found in both popular culture and academic literature, including life course theories, the cohort concept, and the social contract that shapes interactions between generational groups. Readers will understand the strengths and limitations of generational thinking, allowing them to navigate this complex landscape more effectively.

Chapter 5: Who Are Boomers, Gen X, and Gen Y in the Workplace? – A Generational Deep Dive

This chapter is a foundational chapter on the three generational groups at work helping managers grasp their worldviews. An in-depth exploration of Baby Boomers, Generation X, and Millennials provides readers with a nuanced understanding of these groups' behaviors, preferences, and traits. This chapter also offers strategies to work effectively with these cohorts, enhancing collaboration and productivity.

Chapter 6: Who Are Gen Z-ers? – Introducing the New Workforce

This chapter focuses on understanding Generation Z, its attributes, workplace behavior, and expectations. It offers a comparative analysis with older generations and provides the roadmap to understanding how this generation functions. Furthermore, this chapter emphasizes the importance of understanding Generation Z's unique language and communication styles as crucial for building stronger intergenerational relationships within the workplace.

Part II: Hands-On Leadership – Actionable Strategies for Gen Z Integration

Chapter 7: What Are Gen Z-ers' Workplace Expectations and Work Ethic Values? – Decoding Their Professional DNA

This chapter delves into Gen Z's Job Crisis Loop, exploring their career choices and the factors contributing to high turnover. It provides managers with essential knowledge to address these challenges and effectively engage Gen Z talent.

Chapter 8: How to Attract Gen Z Employees in the Workplace – Crafting Appealing Employer Brands

Focusing on employer branding, this chapter guides readers on strategies to attract Gen Z talent. It highlights common pitfalls in employer branding that may deter this cohort, offering practical solutions to build an appealing workplace culture.

Chapter 9: How to Redesign Job Descriptions for Gen Z-ers – Aligning Roles with Aspirations

This chapter addresses how job descriptions and roles can be tailored to meet Gen Z's preferences and skills. Readers will learn from case studies demonstrating effective job design strategies that resonate with Gen Z employees.

Chapter 10: How to Onboard Gen Z Employees – A Structured Approach

This chapter introduces the Gen Z Employee Onboarding and Integration Framework and outlines a comprehensive onboarding process for Gen Z employees. From the initial phase of pre-onboarding, where clear, realistic job descriptions set the stage for success, to the crucial moments of evaluation and assimilation, each stage provides actionable advice crafted to ensure a seamless transition and foster long-term engagement. Key take-aways underscore the necessity of a structured yet flexible onboarding process, the value of mentorship and peer support systems, and the critical role of continuous feedback and professional development.

Chapter 11: Why Are Gen Z Disengaged? – Unearthing the Root Causes

An exploration of the reasons behind Gen Z's disengagement, this chapter introduces the Three Forces of Disengagement and the 3D Disengagement Model. It provides a deep understanding of the factors affecting Gen Z's engagement levels in the workplace. The analysis discusses how power is distributed among the generational groups at work and describes the stark realities of intergenerational interactions and in turn their impact on engagement.

Chapter 12: How to Lead Teams of Gen Z Employees – Adapting Leadership Styles

This chapter offers insights into effective leadership practices for Gen Z teams. It covers various leadership approaches and theories tailored to resonate with the unique characteristics of Generation Z employees. It outlines a strategic blend of Logoleadership, leadership pedagogy, and SuperLeadership complemented with Self-leadership, each underpinned by the necessity for authenticity, meaningful engagement, and a culture of mutual learning and growth.

Chapter 13: How to Empower Gen Z Employees – Addressing Power Dynamics

This chapter explores the issue of empowerment. It discusses Gen Z's perceptions of power in the workplace and offers interventions to create a more empowered and proactive Gen Z workforce. Through research on Gen Z individuals and a comprehensive exploration of power dynamics, readers will understand the situations that lead to their feelings of powerlessness.

Part III: Toolkit for Transformation – Short Guides for Implementation

Chapter 14: What to Do about Quiet Quitting? – Tackling the Gen Z Employee Lifecycle

This chapter investigates the 'quiet quitting' phenomenon within Gen Z, introducing the Employee Lifecycle Curve. It describes the Gen Z employee lifecycle and provides insights into the types and phases of quiet quitters and strategies to mitigate this disengagement. Through the lens of the Exit, Voice, Loyalty, Neglect (EVLN) model, the discussion expands to encompass the broader implications of employee responses to job dissatisfaction, offering leaders an understanding of the dynamics that characterize workforces.

Chapter 15: How to Make Different Generations of Employees Work Together – Maximizing Team Potential

This chapter focuses on actionable techniques for fostering collaboration among diverse age groups within organizations. It begins with essential guidance on forming effective multigenerational teams, emphasizing the value of diversity in team composition. This chapter progresses to strategic task assignments based on individual capabilities and concludes with insights on selecting the right leaders for multigenerational teams.

Chapter 16: How to Implement Multigeneration Training – Fostering Intergenerational Collaboration

Highlighting the importance of training for effective intergenerational collaboration, this chapter presents ideas for overcoming disputes and aligning the strengths of diverse generational groups. It serves as a foundational guide to multigenerational training.

Chapter 17: How to Manage Tensions between Generations – Navigating Workplace Dynamics

This chapter takes an in-depth look at generational tensions and conflict management strategies. It classifies types of tensions and provides solutions for managing conflicts effectively. It serves as a foundational guide for conflict prevention and implementing a conflict management system.

Chapter 18: Eight Actions You Can Take Today – Immediate Steps for Multigenerational Management

This penultimate chapter presents a pragmatic eight-step framework for managing a multigenerational workforce. Designed for CEOs and senior leaders, this checklist offers immediate, actionable steps to enhance engagement, particularly among Gen Z employees, and address widespread disengagement. Each step is outlined with clear recommendations and cautions, ensuring effective implementation for immediate impact in the organization.

Chapter 19: Bonus Chapter The AI-Gen Z Alliance: Redefining Leadership for a New AI Era

This bonus chapter delves into the integration of artificial intelligence (AI) in the workplace and its interaction with Generation Z. This chapter highlights case studies from leading companies, illustrating how AI can enhance leadership and innovation. It provides strategies for leaders to leverage AI for decision-making, talent development, and fostering a culture of continuous learning. This addition to *Gen Z in Work* prepares leaders to navigate the evolving corporate landscape, combining the analytical strengths of AI with the unique characteristics of Generation Z.

Chapter 20: Conclusion – Summarizing the Multigenerational Journey

This concluding chapter synthesizes the key insights and strategies discussed throughout the book. It provides a comprehensive summary of the solutions and frameworks explored in previous chapters, offering readers a clear and concise roadmap for navigating the complexities of the modern, multigenerational workplace.

Box 1.1 From Interviews to Insights: The Research Methodology

The recommendations are grounded in three years of primary mixed-method research, including 75 in-depth interviews with managers and Gen Z employees across various industries. These conversations occurred across 42 companies that set out to unearth Gen Z employees' distinctive qualities and challenges. The research ventured further into the heart of the workplace. A two-year, structured observation of Gen Z personnel tested a series of leadership interventions. This empirical journey led to a framework for managers, dissecting Gen Z's disengagement and offering actionable strategies for transformation.

To the Reader:

This section further discusses the research methodology that under-pins this study. While this detailed exploration will be relevant for researchers, practicing managers focused on implementing solutions may proceed directly to the subsequent chapters for more actionable content.

At the heart of contemporary organizational strategy lies a critical yet often elusive concept: employee engagement. This term reverber-ates through boardrooms and HR departments, underscoring its pivotal role in organizational success. Despite widespread acknowledgment of its importance, a striking paradox exists: the enthusiastic endorsement of employee engagement often lacks a solid foundation in robust qual-itative academic research (Shuck & Wollard, 2010).

This research seeks to reconcile this disparity, embarking on a quest to align organizational aspirations with empirical evidence for meaningful change, mainly focusing on Generation Z in the workplace. The methodol-ogy employed in this research is a mixed-method approach meticulously designed to yield practical insights for business leaders. It bridges the gap between theoretical understanding and real-world application, offering strategies to tackle Generation Z employees' engagement challenges.

The research began with grounded theory,[1] a qualitative research approach renowned for its depth (Charmaz, 2006; Creswell, 2014). This method was instrumental in collecting data from both Generation Z employees and their managers,[2] enabling a holistic comparison of their perspectives on engagement and disengagement (Moustakas, 1994). Data were collected through open-ended, semi-structured interviews in 42 companies across various fields. The study included 75 participants, split into two groups: 30 Generation Z employees and 45 managers. The sample size was determined through theoretical saturation, ensuring diverse viewpoints were captured (Glasser & Strauss, 2017). A non-ran-dom sampling method was utilized, incorporating theoretical and expo-nential non-discriminative snowball sampling techniques (Babbie, 1995; Miller & Crabtree, 1992).

Complementing this, unstructured observation offered an immer-sive view into the day-to-day experiences of ten Generation Z employ-ees within their work environments. Embracing an interpretivist approach, this method aimed to provide rich, detailed descriptions of their workplace experiences (Agar, 1986; Geertz, 1973). A two-year lon-gitudinal study closely monitored the experiences of these employees, uncovering insights into Generation Z's lifecycle, the dynamics of the 'quiet quitting' curve, and typical behaviors indicative of disengage-ment, as well as their responses to leadership interventions.

Data analysis phases encompass bracketing, phenomenological reduction, and axial and selective coding diagramming, ensuring a comprehensive and nuanced understanding of the findings (Hycner, 1999; Martin, 2001; Strauss & Corbin, 1990). Lincoln and Guba's (1985) trustworthiness criteria were employed to guarantee the validity and reliability of the research, encompassing credibility, transferability, dependability, and confirmability. Techniques such as prolonged engagement with participants, triangulation of data sources, thick descriptions, respondent validation, and participant-guided inquiry were utilized to reinforce the study's internal validity (Brown et al., 2002; Cooney, 2010; Jacelon & O'Dell, 2005; Morrow, 2005).

CONCLUSIONS

It is evident that the landscape of the modern workplace is undergoing significant transformation, primarily influenced by the entrance of Generation Z. This new cohort, along with the rapid pace of technological advancement, is reshaping traditional leadership models, compelling a reevaluation of established practices and the adoption of more inclusive strategies that acknowledge the diversity and digital prowess of today's workforce. In addressing these shifts, the text positions itself not merely as a manual but as an imperative for leaders to evolve, innovate, and cultivate environments where the multifaceted potential of every generation can be realized. By comprehensively understanding Generation Z's distinct characteristics and expectations, leveraging artificial intelligence strategically, and championing multigenerational cooperation, organizations can ensure a more engaged, productive, and cohesive workplace, poised to meet challenges and seize future opportunities.

Box 1.2 Key Take-Aways for Chapter 1

1   **Embrace the Gen Z Revolution**: Recognize that the entry of Generation Z into the workforce is not just another generational shift but a transformative movement. This generation brings unique dynamics, and their integration into the workforce requires a fresh

approach. Managers need to understand Gen Z's digital fluency, their aspirations, and how their distinct characteristics can be harnessed to drive productivity and engagement in the workplace;

2 **Develop a Multigenerational Strategy**: Acknowledge the importance of catering to the needs and values of all generational cohorts within the organization. While Gen Z may be the disruptors, a successful organization harmonizes the diverse needs of all employees. Managers should focus on building intergenerational groups and creating a workplace culture that promotes engagement and collaborative synergy across all ages;

3 **Act Now to Address Disengagement**: With a significant portion of the global workforce on the brink of disengagement, particularly among Gen Z employees, it is crucial for managers to act swiftly. Delays in adapting to the multigenerational phenomenon increase the risk of alienating young recruits and exacerbating generational gaps. Proactive measures to engage Gen Z and other generations are essential to prevent further disengagement and maintain a productive workforce.

NOTES

1 Grounded theory is the preferred method to furnish additional value when the literature fails to support the theoretical evolution of phenomena (Charmaz, 2006; Glasser & Strauss, 2017; Moustakas, 1994).

2 See Creswell (2014) on how to develop theory for a particular sample population that possesses potentially valuable variables and characteristics of interest.

REFERENCES

Agar, M. H. (1986). *Speaking of ethnography*. Sage Publications.

Babbie, E. (1995). *The practice of social research* (7th ed.). Wadsworth.

Brown, S. C., Richard, A., Stevens, J., Troiano, P. F., & Schneider, M. K. (2002). Exploring complex phenomenon: Grounded theory in student affairs research. *Journal of College Student Development*, *43*(2), 1–11. https://www.academia.edu/6333193/MARCH_APRIL_2002_u_VOL_43_NO_2_1_Exploring_Complex_Phenomena_Grounded_Theory_in_Student_Affairs_Research

Charmaz, K. (2006). *Constructing grounded theory. A practical guide through qualitative analysis*. Sage.

Cooney, A. (2010). Rigor and grounded theory. *Nurse Researcher, 14*(4), 17–22. https://doi.org/10.7748/nr2011.07.18.4.17.c8631.

Creswell, J. (2014). *Research design* (4th ed.). Sage.

Gallup Inc. (2023). *State of the global workplace: 2023 report.* News Bites - Private Companies. https://search.proquest.com.ezp-prod1.hul.harvard. edu/wire-feeds/gallup-inc-state-global-workplace-2023-report/docview/ 2874596660/se-2

Geertz, C. (1973). Thick description: Toward an interpretive theory of culture. In C. Geertz (Ed.), *The interpretation of cultures: Selected essays* (pp. 3–30). Basic Books. https://cscs.res.in/dataarchive/textfiles/textfile.2009-08-14.211756 2205/file

Glasser, B., & Strauss, A. (2017). *The discovery of grounded theory: Strategies for qualitative research.* Routledge.

Harter, J. (2017). *Dismal employee engagement is a sign of global mismanagement.* https://www.gallup.com/workplace/231668/dismal-employee-engagement-sign-global-mismanagement.aspx

Hycner, R. H. (1999). Some guidelines for the phenomenological analysis of interview data. In A. Bryman & R. G. Burgess (Eds.), *Qualitative research* (Vol. 3, pp. 143–164). Sage.

Jacelon, C. S., & O'Dell, K. K. (2005). Case and grounded theory as qualitative research methods. *Urologic Nursing, 25*(1), 49–52. https://escholarship. umassmed.edu/obgyn_pp/33

James, J., Mckechnie, S., & Swanberg, J. (2011). Predicting employee engagement in an age-diverse retail workforce. *Journal of Organizational Behavior, 32*(2), 173–196. https://doi.org/10.1002/job.681.

Johnson, J. R. (2023). What's new about quiet quitting (and what's not). *The Transdisciplinary Journal of Management.* https://tjm.scholasticahq.com/article/ 72079-what-s-new-about-quiet-quitting-and-what-s-not

Klotz, A. C., & Bolino, M. C. (2022). When quiet quitting is worse than the real thing. *Harvard Business Review.* https://hbr.org/2022/09/when-quiet-quitting-is-worse-than-the-real-thing

Lincoln, Y., & Guba, E. (1985). *Naturalistic inquiry.* Sage.

Martin, R. A. (2001). Humor, laughter, and physical health: Methodological issues and research findings. *Psychological Bulletin, 127*(4), 504–519. https:// doi.org/10.1037/0033-2909.127.4.504.

McGregor, G. (2022). *Before "Quiet Quitting" in the U.S., there was "Lying Flat" in China. How the anti-work movement swept the world's two largest economies.* https://search.ebscohost.com/login.aspx?direct=true&db=bsu&AN=158881425&lang=tr

Miller, W. L., & Crabtree, B. F. (1992). Primary care research: A multimethod typology and qualitative road map. In B. Crabtree & W. Miller (Eds.), *Doing qualitative research* (pp. 3–28). Sage Publications, Inc.

Morrow, S. L. (2005). Quality and trustworthiness in qualitative research in counseling psychology. *Journal of Counselling Psychology, 25*(2), 250–260. https://doi.org/10.1037/0022-0167.52.2.250.

Moustakas, C. (1994). *Phenomenological research methods.* Sage Publications.

Munnell, A. H., Sass, S. A., & Soto, M. (2006). *Employer attitudes towards older workers: Survey results.* Center for Retirement Research at Boston College. https://Crr.Bc.Edu/Images/Stories/ Briefs/Wob_3

Pendell, R., & Vander Helm, S. (2022, November 11). *Generation disconnected: Data on Gen Z in the workplace.* Gallup.Com. https://www.gallup.com/workplace/404693/generation-disconnected-data-gen-workplace.aspx

Pitt-Catsouphes, M., Smyer, M. A., Matz-Costa, C., & Kane, K. (2007). *The National Study Report: Phase II of the national study of business strategy and workforce development.* The Center on Aging & Work/Workplace Flexibility. https://Agingandwork.Bc.Edu/Documents/

Ruggeri, A. (2017). People have always whined about young adults. *The British Broadcasting Corporation.* https://www.Bbc.Com/Capital/Story/20171003-Proof-That-People-Have-Always-Complained-About-Young-Adults

Shuck, B., & Wollard, K. (2010). Employee engagement and HRD: A seminal review of the foundations. *Human Resource Development Review, 9*(1), 89–110. https://doi.org/10.1177/1534484309353560.

Smith, R. A. (2022). Quiet quitters make up half the U.S workforce, gallup says. *Wall Street Journal.* https://www.wsj.com/articles/quiet-quitters-make-up-half-the-u-s-workforce-gallup-says-11662517806

Strauss, A., & Corbin, J. (1990). *Basics of qualitative research: Grounded theory procedures and techniques.* Sage Publications.

WELCOME TO THE MODERN WORKFORCE

Abstract

"Welcome to the Modern Workforce" delves into the significant transformations in today's work environment. This chapter aims to help leaders understand what is happening in the world of work, shaped by rapid technological advancements and changing generational dynamics. It delves into the integration challenges and opportunities presented by a multigenerational workforce, from the experienced Baby Boomers to the emerging Gen Z. This chapter further explores the impact of artificial intelligence (AI) on business operations, emphasizing its dual role as a facilitator of efficiency and a catalyst for strategic innovation. Addressing emerging workplace trends, such as remote work, the gig economy, and the importance of diversity and inclusion, this chapter equips leaders with the necessary terminology, concepts, and insights into adapting to these developments to foster a productive, inclusive, and forward-thinking organizational environment.

THE CURRENT STATE OF WORK: CHANGES AND CHALLENGES

Managers are steering through a radically transformed work landscape in these times of unparalleled change. The past few years have been nothing short of revolutionary, reshaping the contours of the modern workforce. Triggered by the pandemic, a massive shift to

DOI: 10.4324/9781032722696-3

remote work ensued, initially hailed for its productivity, only to encounter skepticism as conflicting studies emerged (Goldberg, 2023). The Great Resignation became apparent in 2021, with employees leaving jobs in significant numbers (Fuller & Kerr, 2022). By the end of 2023, the tables turned as companies initiated workforce reductions. Amidst this, 'quiet quitting' became prevalent, highlighting employees' desires for more flexible work arrangements (Klotz & Bolino, 2022), while companies struggled to engage with the digitally native Gen Z workforce (Pendell & Vander Helm, 2022), leading some to refocus on the more experienced older employees (Fry & Braga, 2023).

Adapting to these changes has not been trivial for managers, with many experiencing burnout (Klinghoffer & Kirkpatrick-Husk, 2023). This is set against the backdrop of the growing integration of artificial intelligence (AI) in the workforce, presenting a double-edged sword: a potential solution to resource challenges for some managers and a threat to job security for others (Anderson & Raine, 2023).

Various age groups' differing experiences and expectations further complicate the workforce landscape. Older workers, for instance, have provided the most favorable job assessments, with two-thirds of those aged 65 and older expressing high satisfaction with their job roles and relationships with managers (Horowitz & Parker, 2023). Meanwhile, Gen Z's preference for virtual work has been met with challenges in their proactivity and engagement levels (Provoke Insights, 2023). Additionally, a notable portion of the workforce, six in ten employees, is reportedly 'quiet quitting,' with over half actively seeking new opportunities (Gallup Inc, 2023). Beyond salary, Gen Z employees are concerned with their employer's image and are often reluctant to advocate for their companies (Statista, 2023). Amidst all managerial changes to better incorporate their preferences, young workers express the lowest levels of job satisfaction (Leppert, 2023).

This evolving workplace environment presents a multifaceted challenge for managers. Balancing the needs of a multigenerational workforce, leveraging the experience of older employees, effectively engaging younger generations, and preparing for the impact of AI are vital considerations.

Box 2.1 Introduction to Who Is Who At Work: A Primary on Generational Groups

To the reader:

This section is the gateway to understanding today's workforce. It lays the groundwork for comprehending different generational groups' distinctive characteristics and expectations, which will be explored in-depth in subsequent chapters.

In an era marked by widespread employee disengagement and the distinct needs of various generations, managers face the challenge of engaging four generational cohorts in the workforce. As of 2022, Generation X and Generation Y will represent 70% of the global workforce. Generation Z is poised to constitute nearly a quarter as they step into their professional roles (Manpower, 2016).

Boomers (born between 1946 and 1964): Occupying many senior roles, Boomers are distinguished by their deep company loyalty and robust work ethic. They firmly believe that success directly results from hard work and are accustomed to postponing immediate rewards for long-term gains. Motivated by financial incentives and a desire to maintain their status within organizational hierarchies, Boomers have left an indelible mark on the professional landscape (Kupperschmidt, 2000; Tolbize, 2008; Twenge et al., 2010).

Generation X (born between 1965 and 1980): This generation combines a solid work ethic with a more fluid sense of company loyalty. Shaped by familial and societal changes, many Gen X-ers have witnessed and adapted to significant fluctuations in their environments. They tend to be skeptical of long-term job commitments, preferring to cultivate their skills and marketability as a form of career security (Kupperschmidt, 2000; Tolbize, 2008; Twenge et al., 2010).

Generation Y (born between 1981 and 1996): Members of this cohort prioritize achieving a balance between their professional and personal lives. Their allegiance to employers is often fluid, and they view jobs as a series of occupational experiences rather than lifelong vocations. This outlook reflects a broader shift in attitudes toward work and career development (Kupperschmidt, 2000; Tolbize, 2008; Twenge et al., 2010).

Generation Z (born after 1996): Entering the workforce with a digital-first mindset, Gen Z professionals are accustomed to immediate feedback and rewards. They tend to be less inclined to put effort beyond their defined roles and are often uncomfortable with traditional workplace hierarchies. They challenge long-standing norms around authority and expect a workplace that aligns more closely with their values and ways of working (Ochis, 2022).

As one delves further into this book, these generational profiles will be crucial for understanding the evolving workplace landscape. They represent not just demographic segments but the changing tides of work attitudes, values, and expectations reshaping how managers think about careers and organizational dynamics.

INTRODUCTION TO EMERGING WORKPLACE TRENDS

In the dynamic business realm, managers are increasingly called upon to navigate and adapt to ever-evolving workplace trends – several of which are being implemented due to generational shifts. The ability to stay informed and agile in these changes is beneficial for those aiming to lead effectively in today's professional environment.

This section aims to equip managers with a comprehensive understanding of the most influential trends currently reshaping organizational dynamics. While managers should not aim to adopt every trend, awareness of their existence and implications is crucial for informed decision-making.

Trends Transforming Today's Workplace

1. **Great Resignation**: A significant shift where employees leave their jobs en masse, seeking better opportunities, enhanced work-life balance, and improved compensation (Fuller & Kerr, 2022).
2. **Quiet Quitting**: Employees cease engaging or contributing at work, withdrawing their participation without formally resigning (Ellis & Yang, 2022).
3. **Quiet Firing** is a subtle process in which employers gradually sideline employees, leading to their eventual departure without a formal termination process.
4. **Ghosting Employers**: Instances where employees abruptly cease all communication and effectively disappear from their roles, leaving without notice or explanation.

5. **Gig Economy**: The rise of independent contractors and free-lancers who offer their services temporarily or on a project basis (Kuhn, 2016).
6. **Remote-First Strategy**: This approach is where remote working is the primary mode of operation, complemented by occasional physical meetings or events (Kossek et al., 2021).
7. **Hybrid Work Model**: This model combines remote work with periodic in-office days, offering employees flexibility in choosing their work setting (Kossek et al., 2021).
8. **Flexible Work Arrangements**: Employers provide employees with options to tailor their work schedules, such as working from home, adjusting work hours, or taking necessary breaks (Kossek et al., 2021).
9. **Activity-Based Working (ABW):** It is a workplace design concept that allows employees to move to different areas suited to their current tasks (Muhonen & Berthelsen, 2021).
10. **Skills-Based Hiring**: A focus on the skills and experiences of candidates rather than solely on their educational background or previous job titles (Fuller & Kerr, 2022).
11. **Culture of Appreciation**: Creating an environment where employee contributions are recognized and valued fosters a positive and engaged workforce.
12. **Well-being Programs**: Investment in programs that support employee well-being, including stress management, fitness initiatives, and mental health resources.
13. **Sustainable Workplace Design**: Incorporating eco-friendly practices in office design and operations, such as using sustainable materials and promoting energy efficiency.
14. **Neurodiversity Hiring**: Embracing the unique strengths and perspectives of individuals with neurocognitive differences in the workforce (Doyle, 2020).
15. **Productivity-Enhancing Spaces**: Designing workspaces that boost productivity with ergonomic furniture, natural lighting, and areas dedicated to focused work.
16. **Wellness-Infused Meetings**: Evolving meeting structures to include well-being elements like physical activity breaks or mindfulness exercises for reduced stress and increased engagement.

17. **FlexBenefits Packages**: Offering employees customizable benefits packages that align with their needs and preferences (Kossek et al., 2021).
18. **Data-Driven Workplace Optimization**: Leveraging data analytics to improve workplace efficiency, focusing on resource allocation, space utilization, and employee satisfaction (Bernhardt et al., 2023).
19. **Diversity, Equity, and Inclusion (DEI) Initiatives**: Committing to creating a more inclusive and equitable workplace through policies and programs that address biases, promote equal opportunities, and celebrate diversity.

These emerging trends are reshaping the landscape of work. For managers and leaders, understanding and adapting to these trends is about staying relevant and harnessing opportunities for organizational growth and employee satisfaction. This awareness is a strategic tool, enabling leaders to make informed decisions and create a resilient, adaptive, and forward-thinking workplace.

EMBRACING AI IN THE MODERN WORKFORCE

To the Reader:

This section delves into the essential AI trends and their far-reaching implications for businesses, offering a comprehensive view of how these technologies fundamentally reshape the workplace. In today's rapidly evolving work environment, technology acts as a primary disruptor, often creating a point of contention across different generational cohorts within the workforce. As leaders grapple with these AI-induced changes, their ability to adeptly navigate this landscape becomes crucial. By embracing AI, they ensure their organizations remain relevant and competitive while opening doors to new possibilities for innovation and growth in a landscape increasingly defined by AI and technology.

Even though some 79% of the canvassed experts said they are more concerned than excited about coming technological change (Anderson & Raine, 2023), it is imperative to recognize that AI is not a fleeting fad but a fundamental shift in businesses' operations. Managers who fail to incorporate AI into their strategies risk falling behind in an increasingly competitive and technology-driven market. The successful integration of AI necessitates a proactive approach, preparing for the technological, cultural, and ethical changes it brings. For instance, Microsoft's (2022) proactive approach to establishing responsible AI practices is a testament to the importance of addressing the ethical dimensions of AI use in businesses.

The evolution of AI in business has shifted from simple automation to enhancing human capabilities. Amazon's transformation from using AI for routine tasks to augmenting human efficiency in warehouses illustrates the true potential of AI – not just as a tool for replacement but as a means to elevate human work (Gantengein, 2020). AI's impact extends beyond technical roles, influencing organizational culture and driving innovation. Salesforce (2024), for instance, integrates AI to bolster decision-making, creating a culture primed for continuous innovation and efficiency.

AI's influence is not limited to operational levels but also transforms leadership. IBM's integration of Watson into executive decision-making showcases AI as a strategic asset, capable of analyzing complex data to inform leadership strategies (Yusuf, 2023). The impact of AI varies based on its application within organizations. For repetitive tasks, AI allows managers more time for strategic work, necessitating training in AI tool management and error handling. When AI is leveraged for insights, managers must have data literacy and analytical skills to interpret AI outputs effectively. AI's integration will lead to cultures emphasizing data-driven decision-making, adaptability, collaboration between humans and machines, and continuous learning.

CONCLUSIONS

In the grand tapestry of the modern workforce, managers and leaders stand at the helm, navigating through a sea of change characterized by technological advancements, shifting generational values, and evolving workplace norms. This chapter illuminates the multifaceted challenges and opportunities presented by these dynamics, underscoring the imperative for leaders to foster an environment of inclusivity, adaptability, and innovation. As the workforce landscape continues to morph, the resilience and foresight of these leaders will determine the trajectory of organizational success and the well-being of their teams. Embracing the diverse talents and perspectives of each generation, from the experienced Baby Boomers to the tech-savvy Gen Z, becomes not just a strategy but a vital element in crafting a cohesive and dynamic organizational culture.

> ### Box 2.2 Key Take-Aways for Chapter 2
>
> 1 **Embrace Generational Diversity**: Actively recognize and cater to the varied needs and work styles of different generations in your team. Implement strategies that bridge the gap between digital natives and experienced professionals, fostering a harmonious and productive work environment.
> 2 **Adapt to Evolving Employment Trends**: Stay responsive to remote and flexible work trends. Balance organizational goals with employees' changing preferences for work-life balance, ensuring productivity and employee satisfaction;
> 3 **Integrate AI Strategically**: Proactively incorporate AI into your business practices. Focus on using AI to enhance efficiency and decision-making while addressing ethical considerations and potential impacts on job security.

REFERENCES

Anderson, J., & Raine, L. (2023, June 21). *As AI spreads, experts predict the best and worst changes in digital life by 2035*. Pew Research Center: Internet, Science & Tech. https://www.pewresearch.org/internet/2023/06/21/as-ai-spreads-experts-predict-the-best-and-worst-changes-in-digital-life-by-2035/

Bernhardt, A., Kresge, L., & Suleiman, R. (2023). The data-driven workplace and the case for worker technology rights. *ILR Review, 76*(1), 3–29. https://doi.org/10.1177/00197939221131558.

Doyle, N. (2020). Neurodiversity at work: A biopsychosocial model and the impact on working adults. *British Medical Bulletin, 135*(1), 108–125. https://doi.org/10.1093/bmb/ldaa021.

Ellis, L., & Yang, A. (2022, August 25). *What is quiet quitting? Employees set boundaries for better work-life balance*. MarketWatch. https://www.marketwatch.com/story/meet-the-so-called-quiet-quitters-i-still-get-just-as-much-accomplished-i-just-dont-stress-and-internally-rip-myself-to-shreds-11661372447

Fry, R., & Braga, D. (2023, December 14). *Older workers are growing in number and earning higher wages.* Pew Research Center's Social & Demographic Trends Project. https://www.pewresearch.org/social-trends/2023/12/14/older-workers-are-growing-in-number-and-earning-higher-wages/

Fuller, J., & Kerr, W. (2022, March 23). The great resignation didn't start with the pandemic. *Harvard Business Review.* https://hbr.org/2022/03/the-great-resignation-didnt-start-with-the-pandemic

Gallup Inc. (2023). *State of the global workplace: 2023 report.* News Bites - Private Companies. https://search.proquest.com.ezp-prod1.hul.harvard.edu/wire-feeds/gallup-inc-state-global-workplace-2023-report/docview/2874596660/se-2

Gantengein, D. (2020, July 7). *Collaboration between Amazon and UC Berkeley advances AI and machine learning.* Amazon Science. https://www.amazon.science/academic-engagements/collaboration-between-amazon-and-uc-berkeley-advances-ai-and-machine-learning

Goldberg, E. (2023, October 10). Here's what we do and don't know about the effects of remote work. *The New York Times.* https://www.nytimes.com/2023/10/10/business/remote-work-effects.html

Horowitz, J., & Parker, K. (2023, March 30). *How Americans view their jobs.* Pew Research Center's Social & Demographic Trends Project. https://www.pewresearch.org/social-trends/2023/03/30/how-americans-view-their-jobs/

Klinghoffer, D., & Kirkpatrick-Husk, K. (2023, May 18). More than 50% of managers feel burned out. *Harvard Business Review.* https://hbr.org/2023/05/more-than-50-of-managers-feel-burned-out

Klotz, A. C., & Bolino, M. C. (2022). When quiet quitting is worse than the real thing. *Harvard Business Review.* https://hbr.org/2022/09/when-quiet-quitting-is-worse-than-the-real-thing

Kossek, E., Gettings, P., & Misra, K. (2021, September 29). The future of flexibility at work. *Harvard Business Review.* https://hbr.org/2021/09/the-future-of-flexibility-at-work

Kuhn, K. (2016). The rise of the "gig economy" and implications for understanding work and workers. *Industrial and Organizational Psychology, 9*(1), 157–162. https://doi.org/10.1017/iop.2015.129.

Kupperschmidt, B. (2000). Multigeneration employees: Strategies for effective management. *The Health Care Manager, 19*(1), 65–76. https://journals.lww.com/healthcaremanagerjournal/Citation/2000/19010/Multigeneration_Employees__Strategies_for.11.aspx

Leppert, R. (2023). *Young workers express lower levels of job satisfaction than older ones, but most are content with their jobs*. Pew Research Center. https://www. pewresearch.org/short-reads/2023/05/25/young-workers-express-lower-levels-of-job-satisfaction-than-older-ones-but-most-are-content-with-their-job/

Manpower. (2016). *Employment worldwide by 2020, by generation*. Statista. https://www-statista-com.ezp-prod1.hul.harvard.edu/statistics/829705/global-employment-by-generation/

Microsoft.com. (2022, June). *Empowering responsible AI practices | Microsoft AI*. https://www.microsoft.com/en-us/ai/responsible-ai

Muhonen, T., & Berthelsen, H. (2021). Activity-based work and its implications for the academic work environment. *Journal of Applied Research in Higher Education, 13*(3), 889–899. https://doi.org/10.1108/JARHE-02-2020-0046.

Ochis, K. (2022, November 28). *Managing the multigenerational workforce. AACSB Insights.* https://www.aacsb.edu/insights/articles/2022/11/managing-the-multigenerational-workforce

Pendell, R., & Vander Helm, S. (2022, November 11). *Generation disconnected: Data on Gen Z in the workplace*. Gallup.Com. https://www.gallup.com/workplace/404693/generation-disconnected-data-gen-workplace.aspx

Provoke Insights. (2023). *Workers who say they are just as productive working virtually as when in the office in the United States in 2022, by generation [Graph. Statista]*. https://www-statista-com.ezp-prod1.hul.harvard.edu/statistics/1350469/productivity-working-from-home-generation-us/

Salesforce.com. (2024, January 23). *AI resource roundup for salesforce admins*. Salesforce Admins. https://admin.salesforce.com/blog/2024/ai-resource-roundup-for-salesforce-admins

Tolbize, A. (2008). *Generational differences in the workplace*. University of Minnesota Press. https://rtc.umn.edu/docs/2_18_Gen_diff_workplace.pdf

Twenge, J., Campbell, S., Hoffman, B., & Lance, C. (2010). *Generational differences in work values: Leisure and extrinsic values increasing, social and intrinsic values decreasing. Journal of Management*. https://doi.org/10.1177/0149206309352246.

Yusuf, K. (2023, May 9). *Introducing watsonx: The future of AI for business*. IBM Blog. https://www.ibm.com/blog/introducing-watsonx-the-future-of-ai-for-business/www.ibm.com/blog/introducing-watsonx-the-future-of-ai-for-business

ARE YOU A MULTIGENERATIONAL LEADER?

Abstract

This chapter explores the challenges and opportunities of managing a diverse workforce, highlighting the importance of Multigenerational Leadership. By understanding and respecting generational differences and fostering a culture of collaboration, managers can unlock the full potential of their teams. The cautionary tale of a call center's generational challenges is a stark reminder of the need for proactive leadership in bridging generational divides. This chapter covers the following sections: Gen Z's Arrival in the Workforce, The Cautionary Tale of GlobalXQ – The Call Centre, Multigenerational Leadership Demystified, Navigating Generational Waters, and The Workplace of the Future Unveiled.

ARE YOU A MULTIGENERATIONAL LEADER? CHECKLIST

To the reader:

By completing this checklist, leaders can gain insights into their effectiveness in managing a multigenerational team and identify areas for growth and development.

1. Generational Awareness:

- ° Do you understand the unique characteristics and preferences of each generation within your team (Baby Boomers, Gen X, Millennials, Gen Z)?

DOI: 10.4324/9781032722696-4

- ° Can you identify generational values, work ethics, and preferences?
- ° Have you evaluated your own biases and perceptions regarding different generations?
- ° Are you aware of how individuals from different generational backgrounds may perceive your leadership style?

2. Inclusive Leadership:

- ° Do you provide training to increase cultural and generational sensitivity and awareness among your staff?
- ° Are you promoting a culture that respects and celebrates diversity in all forms, including age diversity?

3. Communication Strategies:

- ° Do you adapt your communication style to reach and engage team members of different generations effectively?
- ° Are you utilizing multiple communication platforms to meet the diverse preferences of your team?

4. Mentorship and Collaboration:

- ° Do you facilitate mentorship opportunities between different generations within your team?
- ° Are you promoting skill-based collaboration across generations to foster learning and knowledge exchange?
- ° Do you have programs that encourage sharing knowledge and skills across different generations?

5. Professional Development:

- ° Do you provide tailored development opportunities that meet different generations' varying career aspirations and learning styles?
- ° Are you encouraging lifelong learning and upskilling for all team members?
- ° Do you organize multigeneration training?

6. Flexibility and Adaptability:

- ° Do you offer flexible work arrangements that cater to your workforce's diverse needs and preferences?

7. Conflict Resolution:

- ° Can you effectively identify and address intergenerational conflicts within your team?
- ° Do you have a dispute resolution mechanism within your company?

8. Recognition and Rewards:

- ° Do you recognize and reward team members' contributions meaningfully to individuals of different generations?
- ° Are you aware of your team's motivational drivers for each generational cohort?

9. Technological Integration:

- ° Do you leverage technology to enhance team productivity and engagement, considering the tech comfort levels of different generations?
- ° Are you providing training and support to ensure all team members are proficient with new technologies?
- ° Are there platforms or events for younger employees to teach older employees about new technologies and vice versa?

10. Succession Planning:

- ° Have you implemented a succession planning process recognizing employees' potential across different generations?

GEN Z'S ARRIVAL IN THE MULTIGENERATIONAL WORKPLACE

A Gen Z employee, Alex, arrives at work at 9:15 a.m. with an eco-friendly coffee cup and wireless earbuds. They settle at their standing desk adorned with plants and colorful desk toys, sporting a vintage graphic tee and stylish sneakers. Before getting to work, Alex checks their smartphone with pop culture stickers and browses social media to stay updated on trends and memes. As Alex navigates this modern work terrain, they interact with colleagues from different generations, including Baby Boomers. While Boomers, who have a penchant for traditional office routines, occasionally raise eyebrows at Alex's flexible hours and digital-first approach, they admire their tech skills but sometimes struggle to understand the need for constant online connectivity and despise of office chit-chat. Collaborative projects reveal Alex's talent in bridging generational gaps and aiding Boomers in adapting to new technologies.

In the realm of work, Alex is a digital virtuoso, deftly navigating apps and platforms. They prioritize flexibility and autonomy, often opting for remote or coworking spaces. However, when overworked, they remind managers of the contractual hours. Alex's multitasking skills are remarkable, seamlessly switching between work assignments and personal projects. Beyond work, they passionately champion social and environmental causes, organizing fundraisers and volunteering during lunch breaks. Nevertheless, they will not partake in the office parties. Their advocacy for inclusivity and diversity challenges established norms in team meetings.

Deciphering Alex's unique traits and preferences is essential for managing a multigenerational workforce effectively. Balancing their digital savvy, flexibility, and commitment to social causes can unlock their full potential, fostering a dynamic and innovative workplace. However, the reality often differs from this collaborative vision in many businesses, as presented in the following cautionary case study.

Box 3.1 The Cautionary Tale of GlobalXQ – The Call Centre: Navigating Generational Challenges[1]

In the dynamic call center industry, one organization's journey serves as a cautionary tale for businesses seeking younger talent. They decided to offshore a significant part of their operations to tap into fresh Gen Z talent, initially embracing their digital fluency and preference for flexibility. However, this strategic move quickly exposed unforeseen generational challenges, disrupting their operations and culture.

Despite implementing flexible work hours and remote options, the organization faced a startling 40% turnover rate among Gen Z employees in their first three months. For a skilled multigenerational leader, this metric would have indicated a mismatch between job descriptions and the actual work. The Gen Z employees felt they were doing their best to meet key performance indicators (KPIs) but were not rewarded accordingly for doing their best, causing tension with their Gen

X-dominated HR team. Millennials, accustomed to the traditional "Boomer's hustle culture," also perceived preferential treatment for Gen Z.

Boomer team leaders and some industry veterans were reluctant to mentor Gen Z, hindering knowledge sharing and collaboration. Upper management Boomers resisted AI-powered tools, fearing a loss of control to the tech-savvy younger generation. Gen Z employees felt increasingly isolated as time passed, retreating into their smartphones during breaks, further dividing the workplace. A staggering 97% turnover rate among Gen Z hires within a year forced the company to close its offshore operations. The company invested in onboarding and training, assuming a longer retention rate despite metrics showing otherwise.

This cautionary tale emphasizes that attracting young talent with flexible practices – catering to one generation's needs – is just the beginning. Organizations must proactively address generational differences to succeed, fostering mutual understanding, collaboration, and knowledge-sharing. Multigenerational leaders must prioritize creating a harmonious and productive workplace. In the following section, the concept of Multigenerational Leadership is discussed.

MULTIGENERATIONAL LEADERSHIP DEMYSTIFIED

In the realm of contemporary leadership, a palpable sense of urgency envelopes the global businesses, driven by the emergence of younger generations. However, a fog of confusion and apprehension obscures the path ahead. As Deloitte's stark warning underscores, "Entire industries and businesses will rise and fall in the wake of Generation Z. Yet, few industries or organizations seem ready for it" (Deloitte, para 1, 2020). In this context, Multigenerational Leadership[2] takes center stage, illuminating the critical role of managers in navigating this evolving landscape.

Leadership literature finds itself at a crossroads, where the pace of new knowledge does little to surpass the evolution of terminology. In other words, leadership research has left managers to fend for themselves. Multigenerational Leadership springs from the intricate tapestry of employees' characteristics, qualities, behaviors, and preferences spanning diverse generational cohorts (Dwyer & Azevedo,

2016; Kupperschmidt, 2006; Twenge et al., 2010). However, crafting a comprehensive theoretical and practical model based solely on these dimensions proves inadequate. This becomes evident as the exploration delves deeper into understanding the nuanced dynamics that drive engagement. The chapters ahead will reveal that while Boomers, Generation X, and Generation Y shared some commonalities in needs and preferences, the arrival of Gen Z disrupted the equilibrium. Not only were their needs mainly left unexplored until recently, but they also remained largely unaddressed.

Multigenerational Leadership combines leadership with generational thinking, ushering in a fresh perspective. It challenges the status quo in the leader-follower relationship, offering insights into intergenerational conflicts and their profound impact on employee engagement. Simply having a multigenerational team does not automatically make one a multigenerational leader. It demands an understanding of the challenges posed by the values and characteristics of an age-diverse workforce and their consequential influence on engagement and productivity (Dwyer & Azenvedo, 2016). In this paradigm, leaders must deftly navigate the complexities arising from diverse attitudes, human resource practices, organizational changes, and the intricate dance between generations (Dwyer & Azenvedo, 2016). The following list unveils the dynamic dimensions of leadership influenced by generational interplay, shedding light on modern organizational dynamics.

- **Generational Transition Agreements**[3]: As older employees gracefully exit through retirement, astute organizations cultivate the talents of their younger counterparts, meticulously grooming them for pivotal roles within the organizational ecosystem.
- **The Pulse of Societal Evolution**[4]: Multigenerational Leadership thrives on recognizing that generational groups are dynamic entities perpetually influenced by the ever-evolving currents of societal change.
- **Synergy of Collective Ideation and Lifelong Progression**[5]: Each generational group embarks on a distinct life journey fraught with unique challenges at various developmental junctures. By integrating collective wisdom with life course theories, organizations unlock novel pathways to engage and harness the potential of their diverse workforce.

- **The Demographic Nexus**[6]: Embracing the cohort concept as a pivotal demographical unit, Multigenerational Leadership transcends traditional boundaries, weaving a tapestry where each generation's threads intertwine, creating a richer, more vibrant organizational fabric.
- **Navigating the Mosaic of Traits and Influences**: Multigenerational Leadership underscores the divergence in values, preferences, needs, missions, and determinants that define each cohort. By decoding these intricacies, organizations can tailor strategies that resonate with each group, fostering harmonious collaboration and elevating productivity.

To simplify, think of Multigenerational Leadership as encapsulating these five pivotal characteristics:

1. **Values and Needs**: Acknowledging that different generations harbor distinct values, needs, and preferences demanding attention from leadership.
2. **Education**: Prioritizing training and education for employees and managers is the cornerstone of all interactions.
3. **Strengths-Based Approach**: Leveraging each generational group's positive attributes and qualities to enrich the organizational dynamic.
4. **Process-Oriented**: Emphasizing external and internal factors influencing the flow of processes, especially when engaging four generational groups within a single system.
5. **Tensions Management**: Recognizing that a multigenerational workforce inevitably encounters tensions and discerning when intervention is required versus when it is not.

NAVIGATING GENERATIONAL WATERS

Managers trained in the traditional system have probably not experienced this intergenerational renaissance and must now acclimatize to the idea. The resurgence of the topic of generational conflict, with 58% of managers in large organizations with 500 or more reporting tensions between younger and older workers (Cogin, 2012), can be attributed to the transformation of collective identities in an era characterized by individualization and reflexive modernization (Beck, 1997).

This renaissance in generational discourse reflects not only the changing social fabric but also the shifting dynamics of values and expectations across generations (Costanza et al., 2012; Kowske et al., 2010; Smola & Sutton, 2002). Generations, often perceived as classification markers, now play a pivotal role in workplace interactions and beyond (Corsten, 1999). Managers must recognize that each generation learns work expectations through socialization and role negotiation (DeLong, 2004; Marston, 2007; Myers & Sadaghiani, 2010). Without effective management, this negotiation can lead to chaotic workplace cultures that hinder engagement and productivity.

Multigenerational Leadership emerges as the solution to these challenges, demanding a comprehensive understanding of generational differences and a strategic approach to fostering collaboration (R. Dwyer & Azenvedo, 2016; Tapscott, 2009; Zemke et al., 1999). As the business landscape continues to diversify, organizations' success will hinge on the ability of employees from different generations to work together effectively and respectfully. However, achieving this harmony requires confronting stereotypes and generalizations that often overshadow the true potential of intergenerational collaboration (Vance, 2006).

A crucial aspect of Multigenerational Leadership lies in managing power dynamics among generational groups. The absence of organizational systems that promote intergenerational cooperation perpetuates power struggles, with older generations often exerting dominance over their younger counterparts. As managers seek to bridge these divides, they must acknowledge the perspectives of older employees, who may view younger recruits as less responsible, and younger employees, who may feel isolated and overlooked. In the words of young recruits: "There is tension between older and younger employees due to differences in mentality, pedagogical capabilities of older employees, technology use, and work pressure." Alternatively, managers perceive tensions between their young recruits and tenured employees: "Age difference causes tension due to mentality, pedagogical differences, and increased work pressure. Older employees feel superior but less capable with technology, while young employees may lose focus easily."

Box 3.2 The Workplace of the Future Unveiled

To the reader:

This section explores the upcoming changes in the job market. Those who are looking for practical advice may skip this part. However, it may be important for managers to understand the goals of their younger employees as this can help them to adapt to the changing landscape of the organization effectively.

Ten years from now, Alex, the former Gen Z recruit, is now a manager. Their manager's day begins with the seamless integration of AI technology into their daily routine. The AI necklace is an alarm clock and wellness monitor, gently waking them up at the optimal time. It ensures a smooth transition from sleep by syncing with their heartbeat and dispenses a personalized elixir rich in electrolytes to combat mild dehydration.

The AI plays a significant role throughout the morning routine, influencing various aspects of their life, from dietary choices to leisure activities. Technology and human existence are intricately intertwined in this future world, and AI is a constant companion, shaping personal and professional experiences.

In this future landscape, managers like Alex experience a transformed approach to workforce management. AI assistants recruit and onboard Gen Alpha employees, relying on data-driven decisions and gamified tasks to maintain engagement. These employees work from home, supported by their AI assistants and AI HR managers, who offer on-demand guidance and facilitate informal interactions. With automation and AI-driven processes, the traditional concerns of onboarding, retention, and turnover have become a thing of the past, paving the way for a highly efficient and technologically integrated work environment.

CONCLUSIONS

The leadership landscape in today's workforce demands a nuanced understanding and appreciation of various generational cohorts' distinct attributes and needs. Leaders are tasked with leveraging Gen Z's tech-savvy and drive for meaningful work while integrating the experience and knowledge of older generations. This delicate balance requires transforming traditional leadership models to more inclusive, adaptive, and forward-thinking, promoting a culture where every employee feels valued and understood.

Furthermore, the scenario of GlobalXQ illustrates the stark consequences of failing to effectively address and bridge generational divides. The high turnover rates and operational disruptions experienced by the call center underscore the critical need for Multigenerational Leadership. This leadership style transcends age-related stereotypes and fosters a collaborative, respectful, and productive work environment. As businesses continue to confront the rapid pace of technological advancements and shifting workforce dynamics, leaders must cultivate an environment that encourages knowledge-sharing, mentorship, and mutual respect across all age groups. By doing so, they will not only mitigate intergenerational conflicts but also harness the collective strengths of their diverse teams, leading to more significant innovation, employee satisfaction, and organizational success in the ever-evolving work landscape. Multigenerational Leadership is not just an option but a necessity for those seeking to lead their teams to new heights of success and fulfillment.

Box 3.3 Key Take-Aways for Chapter 3

1   **Understand the Multigenerational Workforce**: Recognize that today's workplace comprises multiple generations, each with distinct values, preferences, and needs;

2   **Recognize Generational Differences**: Managers must acknowledge and respect generational differences, from work expectations to communication styles;

3   **Embrace the Principles of Multigenerational Leadership**: Foster an environment where every generation's unique strengths are harnessed, ultimately driving organizational success in an era of generational diversity.

NOTES

1   Names have been changed to maintain confidentiality.
2   See Dwyer and Azenvedo (2016) for a larger discussion on Multigenerational Leadership.

3   See Mannheim's (1952) *The Problem of Generations* for the concept of generation and its influence on social change that precludes the entire body of
research about generation.

4   See Ortega y Gasset's (1933) concept of generations from a temporal lens.

5   See Erikson's sequence of human development for a discourse on maturation stages.

6   See the age as a classification concept stating that "birth cohorts are collective aggregates of socially structured life histories" (Corsten, 1999, p. 250).

REFERENCES

Cogin, J. (2012). Are generational differences in work values fact or fiction:
Multi-country evidence and implications. *International Journal of Human Resource
Management, 23,* 2268–2294. https://doi.org/10.1080/09585192.2011.

Corsten, M. (1999). The time of generations. *Time & Society, 8*(2), 249–272.
https://doi.org/10.1177/0961463X99008002003.

Costanza, D., Badger, J., Fraser, R., Severt, J., & Gade, P. (2012). Generational
differences in work-related attitudes: A meta-analysis. *Journal of Business Psychology, 27*(4), 375–394. https://doi.org/10.1007/s10869-012-9259-4.

Deloitte. (2020). *Welcome to Generation Z. Network of executive women.* file:///C:/
Users/HP/Desktop/welcome-to-gen-z.pdf

DeLong, D. W. (2004). *Lost knowledge: Confronting the threat of an aging workforce.*
Oxford University Press.

Dwyer, R., & Azenvedo, A. (2016). Preparing leaders for the multi-generational
workforce. *Journal of Enterprising Communities People and Places in the Global
Economy, 10*(3), 10 1108-08-2013-0025.

Dwyer, R. J., & Azevedo, A. (2016). Preparing leaders for the multi-generational
workforce. *Journal of Enterprising Communities: People and Places in the Global
Economy, 10*(3), 281–305. https://doi.org/10.1108/JEC-08-2013-0025.

Kowske, B. J., Rasch, R., & Wiley, J. (2010). Millennials' (lack of) attitude
problem: An empirical examination of generational effects on work attitudes.
Journal of Business and Psychology, 25(2), 265–279. https://doi.org/10.1007/
S10869-010-9171-8.

Kupperschmidt, B. (2006). Addressing multigenerational conflict: Mutual
respect and carefronting as strategy. *OJIN: The Online Journal of Issues in Nursing, 11*(2). https://doi.org/10.3912/OJIN.Vol11No02Man03.

Mannheim, K. (1952). The problem of generations. In M. K (Ed.), *Essays on the sociology of knowledge* (pp. 276–322). Routledge. https://Archive.Org/Details/Essaysonsociolog00mann

Marston, C. (2007). *Motivating the "what's in it for me?" workforce: Manage across the generational divide and increase profits.* John Wiley & Sons, Inc.

Myers, K. K., & Sadaghiani, K. (2010). Millennials in the workplace: A communication perspective on millennials' organizational relationships and performance. *Journal of Business and Psychology, 25*(2), 225–238. https://doi.org/10.1007/s10869-010-9172-7.

Ortega, & Gasset, J. (1933). *The modern theme.* Northon.

Smola, K. W., & Sutton, C. (2002). Generational differences: Revisiting generational work values for the new millennium. *Journal of Organizational Behavior, 23*(4), 363–382. https://www.Jstor.Org/Stable/4093812

Tapscott, D. (2009). *Grown up digital: How the net generation is changing your world* (1st ed.). Mcgraw-Hill.

Twenge, J., Campbell, S., Hoffman, B., & Lance, C. (2010). Generational differences in work values: Leisure and extrinsic values increasing, social and intrinsic values decreasing. *Journal of Management, 36*(5), 1117–1142. https://doi.org/10.1177/014920630935224.

Vance, R. J. (2006). *Employee engagement and commitment.* Society for Human Resource Management. https://www.shrm.org/hr-today/trends-and-forecasting/special-reports-and-expert-views/documents/employee-engagement-commitment.pdf

Zemke, R., Raines, C., & Filipczak, B. (1999). Generations at work: Managing the clash of Veterans, Boomers. In *Xers, and Nexters in your workplace* (1st ed.). Amacom.

WHAT IS A GENERATION AT WORK?

Abstract

This chapter explores the concept of generations. It clarifies prevailing concepts in popular culture and academic literature, including life course theories, the cohort concept, and the social contract that shapes interactions between generational groups. Readers will understand the strengths and limitations of generational thinking, allowing them to navigate this complex landscape more effectively.

WHY HAS "GENERATIONAL TALK" TAKEN CENTER STAGE IN WORKPLACE DISCUSSIONS?

Generational theories offer a lens through which we can understand the evolving landscape of the workforce. These theories chart the historical journey of human and workplace dynamics and cultural shifts. Corsten (1999) notes a resurgence in generational discourse sparked by the quest for identity in a rapidly changing global society.

> The topic of generation has experienced a renaissance in the last five to ten years. The most important reason for this development is the crisis of collective identities, which is due to a number of circumstances and conditions […] generations and age seem to be new classification markers […] in effect this means that, assuming standardized life courses, birth cohorts are collective aggregates of socially structured life histories.
>
> (Corsten, 1999, p. 250)

DOI: 10.4324/9781032722696-5

Factors driving this interest include the rise of individualism, the fading of traditional societal conflicts, and the questioning of historical ideologies (Beck, 1997; Fukuyama, 1989). This backdrop sets the stage for a deeper exploration of what constitutes a generation within the professional realm.

DEFINING "GENERATION": MORE THAN JUST AGE

What exactly is a "generation"? The term carries multiple dimensions:

1. Generation as lineage,
2. Generation as a group sharing the same historical life space,
3. Generation as a stage of life, and
4. Generation as a unique era (Kertzer, 1983).

This multifaceted definition prompts us to consider generations beyond mere age groups, inviting a richer understanding of each cohort's unique perspective.

THE ETERNAL CYCLE: GENERATIONS IN FLUX

There are no spontaneous generations but a series of generations. The philosopher Ortega y Gasset (1933) claims that a generation "is the most important conception in history" (p. 15). The profound reflection underscores the relentless march of time and its impact on society and history. This concept reveals the cyclical nature of generations, shaped by the era they inhabit and, in turn, shaping the cultural and social milieu for the next. Mannheim (1952) expands on this, illustrating how generational shifts impact societal structures and necessitate the continual passing of cultural and institutional knowledge.

The following five characteristics of social life processes ensure:

1. "New participants in the cultural process are emerging;
2. Former participants in the process are continually disappearing;
3. Members of any one generation can participate only in a limited section of the historical process;
4. It is thus necessary to continually transmit the accumulated cultural heritage; and

5. The transition from generation is a continuous process" (Mannheim, 1952, p. 292).

GENERATIONS IN THE CORPORATE WORLD: A MICROCOSM OF SOCIETY

The corporate environment is not insulated from these broader societal shifts. In any organization, employees come and go, carrying the legacy of the company's culture and contributing to its ongoing evolution. Newcomers bring fresh perspectives and ideas, while seasoned veterans offer wisdom and historical context. This dynamic interplay ensures the continuous transmission of knowledge and values, which is crucial for the sustained success and adaptability of the business.

HOW EXACTLY DOES A GENERATION COME INTO BEING?

Mannheim (1952) illuminates by stating, "Individuals who belong to the same generation, who share the same year of birth, are endowed, to that extent, with a common location in the historical dimension of the social process" (p. 290). This statement lays the foundation for understanding that generations are not arbitrary divisions but groups shaped by shared historical and social experiences.

According to Mannheim (1952), a generation's collective cohesion is evident on three levels: generational site, generational actuality, and generational units, which are further explained and exemplified in Table 4.1.

These layers help explain how individuals born around the same time and experiencing similar events form a cohesive generational identity. Yet, scholars like Ryder (1965) have challenged the clarity of this definition, arguing that the fluidity of these terms can muddy the analytical waters. Since Ryder (1965), generational cohorts have become demographical units used today in academia and popular culture.

Furthermore, Erikson's (1982) theory on human development stages introduces the concept of life stages intersecting with generational identity, adding another dimension to our understanding of

Table 4.1 Levels of Generations

Level	Description	Explanation	Examples
Generational site	Like the concept of classes, people born in a certain period in a geographically limited space are focused on the structure of opportunity.	People born in the same period experience historical events in a similar sequence in their lifetime and events that occur in the same historical phase in the same specific biographical order.	People born in Germany in 1940 experienced the World War II in early childhood, reconstruction in their youth, prosperity in early adulthood, and a stagnation crisis in middle age.
enerational actuality	The experiences of a generation are connected by interpreta-tion.	The collective arranges its experiences through primary intentions and principles of construction.	People born around 1929 were described as the skeptical generation by describing the 60s movement as Melancholy.
Generational units	Concrete groups of people of the same age similarly define their situation and develop similar ways of reacting to their generational problems.	An intra-*differentia-tion* of one generational context into several possibly hostile or rival generational units emerges.	Segmentation of the 60s move-ments into hippies and rockers.

Source: Adapted from Corsten (1999).

how generational characteristics emerge. Erickson (1982) approaches maturity as a process formed through stages. Within each stage, the person faces a crisis or dilemma that the person must resolve to move forward to the next stage or not resolve, which results in incomplete development (Erikson, 1982). The same can be said of an employee lifecycle.

DECODING GENERATIONAL ARCHETYPES: STRAUSS AND HOWE'S FRAMEWORK

Strauss and Howe (1991) broadly define generational cohorts, introducing a cyclical model that has significantly influenced the view on generational differences. Despite the controversy, their framework offers a structured approach to deciphering each generational group's unique traits and shared experiences. They propose that societal events and cultural shifts carve out distinct generational archetypes. The Strauss–Howe generational theory identifies a recurring generational cycle in American history, albeit it is claimed as viable for most countries (Strauss & Howe, 1991). Strauss and Howe (1991) define a social generation as the aggregate of all people born over roughly 20 years. Generations are identified, from first birthyear to last, by looking for cohort groups of this length that share three criteria: age and location in history, common beliefs and behaviors, and perceived membership to the generation (Strauss & Howe, 1991). Childhood and young adulthood produce four generational archetypes that repeat sequentially, in rhythm with generational events (Strauss & Howe, 1997). Archetypes, as well as their characteristics, are exhibited in Table 4.2.

Table 4.2 Generational Archetypes

Archetype	*Prophet*	*Nomad*	*Hero*	*Artist*
Generations	Baby Boomer (1943–1960)	Generation X (1961–1981)	Millennial (1982–2000)	Homeland (2005-present)
Turning	**Awakening**	**Unraveling**	**Crises**	**High**
Reputation as child	Spirited	Bad	Good	Placid
Coming of age	Sanctifying	Alienating	Empowering	Unfulfilling
Primary focus coming of age	Inner-world	Self-sufficiency	Outer-world	Inter-dependency
Young adulthood	Reflecting	Competing	Building	Improving

(*Continued*)

Table 4.2 (Continued)

Archetype	Prophet	Nomad	Hero	Artist
Transition in midlife	Detached to judgmental	Frenetic to exhausted	Energetic to hubristic	Conformist to experimental
Leadership style entering elderhood	Righteous, austere	Solitary, pragmatic	Collegial, expansive	Pluralistic, indecisive
Reputation as elder	Wise	Tough	Powerful	Sensitive
Treatment as elder	Respected	Abandoned	Rewarded	Liked
How is it nurtured	Relaxing	Under-protective	Tightening	Overprotective
Positive reputation	Principled, resolute, creative	Savvy, practical, perceptive	Selfless, rational, competent	The caring, open-minded, expert
Negative reputation	Narcissistic, presumptuous, ruthless	Unfeeling, uncultured, amoral	Unreflective, mechanistic, overbold	Sentimental, complicated, indecisive
Endowments	Vision, values, religion	Liberty, survival, honor	Community, affluence, technology	Pluralism, expertise, due process

Source: Adapted from Strauss and Howe (1997).

Navigating the Labyrinth of Generational Labels

While widespread, the process of labeling generations is fraught with inconsistencies and cultural biases. Standard terms, such as "Millennials" or "Generation X," stem primarily from popular media and culture, leading to a mismatch in global contexts. Moreover, the debate over the precise years that define each generation adds another layer of complexity to understanding generational identities, as seen in Table 4.3.

Table 4.3 Generational labeles cited in defferent sources

	Silent Generation 1925–1943	Boom Generation 1943–1960	13th Generation 1961–1981	Millennial Generation 1982–2000	Homeland Generation 2005–present
Howe and Strauss, (1991)	Silent Generation 1925–1943	Boom Generation 1943–1960	13th Generation 1961–1981	Millennial Generation 1982–2000	Homeland Generation 2005–present
Lancaster and Still-man, (2002)	Traditionalists 1900–1945	Baby Boomers 1946–1964	Generation Xers 1965–1980	Millennials / Generation Y / Generation Next 1981–1999	
Martin and Tulgan (2002)	Silent Generation 1925–1942	Baby Boomers 1946–1960	Generation X 1965–1977	Millennials 1978–2000	
Oblinger and Oblinger (2005)	Matures <1946	Baby Boomers 1947–1964	Gen Xers 1965–1980	Gen Y / NetGen / Millennials 1981–1995	Post Millennials 1995–present
Tapscott (1998)		Baby Boomers 1946–1964	Generation X 1965–1975	Digital Gen / NetGen 1976–2000	
Zemke et al. (1999)	Veterans 1922–1943	Baby Boomers 1943–1960	Generation Xers 1960–1980	Nexters 1980–1999	
Sessa et al. (2007)	Swingers/Silents 1934–1945	Baby Boomers 1940–1946	Generation Xers 1960–1982	Millennials / Generation Yers / NetGen 1982–present	

Source: Adapted from Reeves and Oh (2008).

Box 4.1 Current Labels of Generational Groups

Most contemporary theorists and practitioners used to follow the categorizations provided by the Pew Research Center.

1   Boomers birth years: 1946–1964;
2   Generation X birth years: 1965–1980;
3   Millennials/Generation Y birth years: 1981–1996; and
4   Generation Z birth years: 1997–2012 with no specified end point (Dimock, 2019).

Box 4.2 Disclaimer on Generational Group Labeling

To the reader:
Managers and business leaders should approach the topic of generational labels with a critical eye. This section, while dense with theoretical underpinnings, highlights the nuances and potential pitfalls in generational research. Managers should be mindful of these complexities when applying generational theory in practice, recognizing the individuality within each generational cohort and the cultural specificity of generational experiences.

The concept of generations in the workplace has evolved significantly since Mannheim's (1952) documentary process. This work shifted focus from purely biological perspectives to a more nuanced understanding of social and historical impacts on generational behavior. Nevertheless, the application of generational theory in business has its controversies. Critiques, notably from Rudolph et al. (2020), highlight a speculative trend in popular generational research, pointing out the lack of reliable data backing many widely accepted generational theories, particularly those of Strauss and Howe (1991). This lack of reliability stems from the blurred lines between generations and the influence of other time-bound variables.

When it comes to defining generations, experts do not agree. The disagreement extends from the names of different generations to the specific events influencing each one and the years encompassing each one. Research findings, like those from Smola and Sutton (2002) and (Costanza et al., 2012), show significant variations in defining generational start and end dates, leading to inconsistencies in business and leadership literature (Rudolph et al., 2018). This inconsistency complicates the application of generational theory in organizational settings, as Rudolph et al. (2018) noted.

These discrepancies are not just academic – they have real-world implications for managers. The challenge intensifies when you consider the global workplace. Generational labels predominantly originate from US culture and may not resonate in other cultural contexts. For example, terms like "Millennials" hold less meaning in non-Western settings, where generations might be defined by local historical or cultural milestones, such as wars or political changes (Deal et al., 2010).

In practice, this means not relying solely on US-centric generational labels but instead seeking to understand employees' unique experiences and perspectives from different cultural backgrounds. For instance, aligning with Weiss and Zhang (2020), managers might adapt generational labels to reflect significant local events or societal changes relevant to their teams' cultural contexts yet employ US date ranges. A second approach has been to develop country-specific generational groups based on local events that impacted people in that country and a third and most prominent approach has been to eschew the issue and use US-based generational labels and years when studying individuals in other countries.

CONCLUSIONS

In conclusion, for managers and business practitioners, understanding this concept of generations is essential for fostering a harmonious and productive work environment.

This chapter underlines the significance of generational theories, offering a historical perspective that underscores the evolution of generational concepts over time. The discussion highlights the importance of generational cohorts in understanding the dynamics of organizational settings, presenting an opportunity for managers to harness the strengths of each generation.

The definition of a generation extends beyond mere age groups to encompass kinship, cohort experiences, life stages, and historical periods. This multifaceted view encourages managers to consider the diverse backgrounds and experiences that employees bring to the table.

As posited by Ortega y Gasset, the unwritten rule of generations underscores the continuous cycle of life, with new individuals entering the cultural process as former participants exit. This perpetual motion is mirrored in the workplace, where transmitting company culture and processes from generation to generation is crucial for sustainability and growth.

Moreover, the generational archetypes proposed by Strauss and Howe provide a framework for understanding generational groups' varying needs, values, and behaviors. Managers can leverage this knowledge to tailor their leadership and communication styles to meet the unique needs of each generation. This chapter further explores how generations "happen," highlighting the role of everyday experiences and shared histories in shaping generational identities. This understanding is crucial for managers aiming to create a cohesive team environment that respects and integrates diverse generational perspectives.

Box 4.3 Key Take-Aways for Chapter 4

1 **Challenge Stereotypes and Move Beyond Labels:** Understand generational characteristics but do not box your employees into age-based stereotypes. Acknowledge the diverse individual experiences that exist within each age group;

2 **Generations are Here to Stay:** See generational differences not as obstacles but as opportunities. Work actively to create a workplace that values and integrates the varied experiences and skills of all age groups. Generations are not a fad but an integral part of an organization's lifecycle;

3 **Understand the Spectrum of Generational Theory:** Acknowledge that generational categories are not rigid or universally applicable. With a deeper understanding of the nuances behind generational theories, managers should recognize that a complex mix of influences shapes each generation.

REFERENCES

Beck, U. (1997). The social morals of an individual life. *Cultural Values, 1*(1), 118–126. https://doi.org/10.1080/14797589709367137.

Corsten, M. (1999). The time of generations. *Time & Society, 8*(2), 249–272. https://doi.org/10.1177/0961463X99008002003.

Costanza, D., Badger, J., Fraser, R., Severt, J., & Gade, P. (2012). Generational differences in work-related attitudes: A meta-analysis. *Journal of Business Psychology, 27*(4), 375–394. https://doi.org/10.1007/s10869-012-9259-4.

Deal, J. J., Altman, D. G., & Rogelberg, S. G. (2010). Millennials at work: What we know and what we need to do (if anything). *Journal of Business and Psychology, 25*(2), 191–199. https://doi.org/10.1007/s10869-010-9177-2.

Dimock, M. (2019). *Defining generations: Where millennials end and Generation Z begins.* https://www.pewresearch.org/fact-tank/2019/01/17/where-millennials-end-and-generation-z-begins/

Erikson, E. H. (1982). *The life cycle completed: A review.* Norton.

Fukuyama, F. (1989). The end of history? *The National Interest, 16,* 3–18. https://www.jstor.org/stable/24027184

Kertzer, D. (1983). Generation as a sociological problem. *Annual Reviews, 9,* 125–149. https://is.muni.cz/el/fss/podzim2013/SOC573/um/Kertzer.pdf

Mannheim, K. (1952). The problem of generations. In K. Mannheim (Ed.), *Essays on the Sociology of Knowledge* (pp. 276–322). Routledge. https://Archive.Org/Details/Essaysonsociolog00mann

Ortega, & Gasset, J. (1933). *The modern theme.* Northon.

Reeves, T., & Oh, E. (2008). Generational differences. In S. Spector, D. Merrill, J. Merrienboer, & M. Driscoll (Eds.), *Handbook of Research on Educational Communications and Technology* (3rd ed., pp. 295–303). Taylor & Francis Group.

Rudolph, C. W., Rauvola, R., & Zacher, H. (2018). Leadership and generations at work: A critical review. *The Leadership Quarterly, 29*(1), 44–57. https://doi.org/10.1016/j.leaqua.2017.09.004.

Ryder, N. (1965). The cohort as a concept in the study of social change. *American Sociological Review, 30*(6), 843–861. https://doi.org/10.2307/2090964.

Smola, K. W., & Sutton, C. D. (2002). Generational differences: Revisiting generational work values for the new millennium. *Journal of Organizational Behavior, 23*(SpecIssue), 363–382. https://doi.org/10.1002/job.147.

Strauss, W., & Howe, N. (1991). *Generations: The history of America's future, 1584 to 2069.* Harper Perennial. https://archive.org/stream/GenerationsTheHistoryOfAmericasFuture1584To2069ByWilliamStraussNeilHowe/Generations+The+History+of+America%27s+Future%2C+1584+to+2069+by+William+Strauss+%26+Neil+Howe_djvu.txt

Strauss, W., & Howe, N. (1997). *The fourth turning: An American prophecy—What the cycles of history tell us about America's next rendezvous with destiny.* Broadway Books.

Weiss, D., & Zhang, X. (2020). Multiple sources of aging attitudes: Perceptions of age groups and generations from adolescence to old age across China, Germany, and the United States. *Journal of Cross-Cultural Psychology, 51*(6), 407–423. https://doi.org/10.1177/0022022120925904.

WHO ARE BOOMERS, GEN X, AND GEN Y IN THE WORKPLACE?

Abstract

This foundational chapter explores Baby Boomers, Generation X, and Millennials, providing readers with a nuanced understanding of these groups' behaviors, preferences, and traits. It identifies critical determinants shaping each cohort. The text offers strategic insights for managers to effectively lead different generations, emphasizing the necessity of tailored approaches. It highlights the significance of understanding generational differences in fostering workplace collaboration and productivity.

GENERATIONS AT A GLANCE

To the Reader:

This chapter comprehensively answers three critical questions at the top of today's business leaders' minds: (1) Who are the Baby Boomers, Generation X, and Millennials? (2) What distinct work preferences define each group? (3) How do these cohorts vary in their expectations of leadership?

To effectively differentiate between generational cohorts, one must first understand the defining characteristics of each group, which may be determined through a six-point framework:

1. A formative or traumatic event;
2. Significant demographic changes;
3. Periods linked to the group's collective success or failure;

DOI: 10.4324/9781032722696-6

4. The establishment of a "sacred space" that preserves collective memory;
5. Influential mentors or heroes, contrasted by antiheroes; and
6. A community of individuals who share support and knowledge (Wyatt, 1993).[1]

Applying Wyatt's (1993) framework, the distinct characteristics that define Baby Boomers and Generations X and Y are elaborated in Table 5.1. Essentially, this framework represents how each generational group perceives the world. To effectively engage with diverse generational groups, a manager must endeavor to understand and appreciate the world from cohorts' unique perspectives.

Tailoring strategies to engage and motivate an increasingly diverse workforce demands a nuanced understanding of each generational cohort's values and expectations. For Millennials, this might involve crafting roles that offer significant flexibility and imbue a sense of purpose. For Generation X, success may be found in cultivating an environment where meritocracy and individual contributions are recognized and rewarded. Meanwhile, Baby Boomers are likely to be most engaged by leadership that champions share objectives and reinforce a sense of organizational fidelity.

Work values are significantly shaped by generational experiences rather than merely by age or stages of maturation (Smola & Sutton, 2002). The diverse challenges, societal norms, and historical events encountered by each generation lead to unique work-related preferences and expectations as individuals advance throughout their careers.[2] This chapter delves into these aspects, illustrated foundationally in Table 5.2, providing an initial understanding that will equip leaders to grasp the complexities of today's multigenerational workforce.[3]

THE BOOMER LEGACY: PIONEERS OF CHANGE

The Baby Boomer generation experienced their formative years during significant economic and educational growth. This backdrop fostered a sense of entitlement and high expectations for life achievements, profoundly influencing their work ethics and values. Educated under a traditional system characterized by rigorous standards and a strong emphasis on collaboration and the humanities, Boomers

Table 5.1 Determinants of Generational Groups

	Formative Event	Shift In Demogra-phy	Interval	Sacred Space	Heroes / Anti-Heroes	Work of People Who Support Each Other
Boomers	Vietnam War (Wyatt, 1993)	Baby Boom: Spring in birth rates (Wyatt, 1993)	Sexual revolution; The Civil Rights and Women's Movements; Working Class Decline (Wyatt, 1993)	Woodstock (Wyatt, 1993)	Martin Luther King; Malcom X; The Kennedys; Lee Harvey Oswald (Wyatt, 1993)	George Lucas, Bruce Springsteen, Sam Shepard, Michael Herr.
Generation X	Gulf War; End of Cold War; AIDS Challenger Space Shuttle	Baby Bust; Low Birth Rates	Global Financial Crisis; Decline of totalitarian regimes	Silicon Valley	Donald Trump, Nelson Mandela, and Tom Cruise	Bill Gates, Steve Jobs
Generation Y	9/11; Terrorism Hurricane Katrina;	Echo boom (PEW, 2015); Relocation; Remote work; Feminism	Global Financial Crisis of 07–08 (PEW, 2018); Fourth Industrial Revolution	Internet; Coachella	Justin Trudeau Barack Obama Influencers	Reality TV stars Mark Zuckerberg, Elon Musk

Table 5.2 Work Orientations of Boomers Gen X and Gen Y

Generation	Boomers	Gen Xers	Gen Yers
Training	Too much, and I will leave	Required to keep me	Continuous and expected
Learning style	Facilitated	Independent	Collaborative and networked
Communication	Guarded	Hub and spoke	Collaborative
Problem-solving	Horizontal	Independent	Collaborative
Decision-making	Team Informed	Team included	Team decided
Leadership style	Get out of the way	Coach	Partner
Feedback	Once per year	Weekly/Daily	On-demand
Technology use	Unsure	Unable to work without it	Unfathomable if not provided
Job changing	Sets me back	Necessary	Part of my daily routine
Retirement	Retool	Renew	Recycle

Source: Adapted from Lancaster and Stillman (2003).

developed a respect for structure, teamwork, and intellectual development from an early age (Tolbize, 2008). Their adult years were marked by social changes, including the redefinition of gender roles and family structures, alongside widespread societal upheaval. These experiences cultivated a generation of idealists and activists passionate about civil rights and social causes (Smola & Sutton, 2002).

Boomers are often characterized as workaholics and strong-willed, with a focus on work content and material success. They typically value hierarchical recognition, such as promotions and corner office spaces, indicative of their commitment and achievements. However, the economic recessions and widespread organizational restructuring challenged their loyalty and reshaped their perceptions of job security and corporate fidelity (Kupperschmidt, 2000). Baby Boomers emerged as "free agents" in the workplace, advocating for individual rights and prioritizing personal needs over collective goals. This mindset shifted the corporate landscape, pushing businesses to meet the demand for a more personalized economy and work environment, rewarding innovation and immediate results over loyalty and long-term planning (Smola & Sutton, 2002)

Boomers often find themselves balancing the care of aging parents with responsibilities toward their children, many facing the effects of marital instability and shifting family dynamics (Kupperschmidt, 2000). Despite these challenges, they bring significant strengths to the workplace, such as consensus building, mentoring, and a capacity for driving change. As they navigate the later stages of their careers, many Boomers reevaluate their definitions of work and success, seeking simplicity and fulfillment beyond traditional work metrics.

Tolbize (2008) notes a distinct contrast in training preferences between generations. Older workers, like Boomers, favor skills training within their expertise areas. This contrasts with younger generations, who lean towards leadership and soft skills development, often through informal feedback rather than structured programs.

GEN X UNLEASHED: THE BRIDGE GENERATION

Generation Xers, shaped by their upbringing during societal and familial instability, exhibit a unique blend of individualism and adaptability. Jurkiewicz and Brown (1998) note their tendency towards individualism over collectivism, a trait developed from growing up in environments marked by financial insecurity, rapid societal changes, and the lack of stable traditions. The increase in dual-income households and higher divorce rates (Karp et al., 1999; Kupperschmidt, 2000) led many in this cohort to seek support within tight-knit groups of friends, favoring small, supportive enclaves over traditional family structures.

Their childhood experiences – including soaring national debts, an educational focus on social skills over academics, and a rise in diverse family dynamics – have forged Gen Xers into resourceful, independent individuals who are adept at multitasking and comfortable with diversity (Jurkiewicz & Brown, 1998; Kupperschmidt, 2000). Accustomed to the instant feedback of digital technology and growing up amidst the rise of personal computing, Gen Xers bring a pragmatic, problem-solving approach to the workplace, marked by their technical competence and adaptability to change (O'Bannon, 2001).

Their professional expectations differ markedly from those of previous generations. Having witnessed the instability of their parents' careers, they are inherently skeptical and value job flexibility, technological advancement, and opportunities for personal development over traditional job security (Kupperschmidt, 2000). They seek a balance between work and leisure and demand that work be engaging and rewarding (O'Bannon, 2001). Contrary to being the slackers they were once dubbed, Gen Xers are prepared to work hard but on their terms, which often include a demand for competent management, continuous learning, and a precise alignment between their values and those of their employer (Jurkiewicz & Brown, 1998; Kupperschmidt, 2000).

Their critical nature and independence can sometimes be perceived as resistance to authority, posing challenges for traditional management styles. However, Gen X employees value transparent communication and leadership that mentors rather than micromanages. As they strongly emphasize practicality and current relevance, Gen X employees prioritize alignment with organizations that recognize their skills, reward productivity, and foster a community feeling rather than mere organizational loyalty (Kupperschmidt, 2000; O'Bannon, 2001).

Understanding and leveraging the strengths of Generation X involves acknowledging their unique background, addressing their demands for a balanced and meaningful work life, and providing them with an environment that values their independence while offering stable, supportive leadership. Managers are tasked with creating inclusive, adaptable workplaces that respect the competencies and personal needs of Gen Xers, thereby fostering mutual alignment with organizational goals (Jurkiewicz & Brown, 1998; Kupperschmidt, 2000; O'Bannon, 2001).

MILLENNIAL MOMENTUM: SHAPING THE FUTURE

Despite the mixed and often contradictory research, certain aspects regarding their work attitudes, technology usage, and work ethic have been well-documented. Millennials are often characterized by a desire for work-life balance, a trend possibly inherited from Generation X's preferences but amplified by their unique circumstances (Smola & Sutton, 2002; Twenge et al., 2010). Millennials have ushered in a new era in the workplace, characterized by evolving attitudes towards work, an intrinsic relationship with technology, and a reshaped concept of work ethic influenced by economic and societal shifts. Following Generation X, who sought higher salaries and flexible work arrangements, Millennials have intensified these demands, advocating for even more adaptable and rewarding work environments (Jennings, 2000). Their digital nativity enables them to remain connected constantly, fostering a workplace dynamic where access to information and communication is uninterrupted (Ryan, 2000).

This generation's upbringing, marked by economic instability and observing their parents' job insecurities, has culminated in skepticism towards traditional institutions, similar yet distinct from their Generation X predecessors. However, Millennials distinguish themselves through a pronounced willingness to voice their opinions and a robust inclination toward social advocacy. Their desire to effect social change aligns them with the activist spirit of the 1960s, signaling a potential for heightened social engagement within and beyond the workplace (Ryan, 2000).

Despite prevailing stereotypes of entitlement or disinterest in hard work, research suggests that Millennials' work patterns are not substantially different from those of prior generations when adjusted for age and economic context (Staff & Schulenberg, 2010). They value meaningful work and exhibit similar altruistic values, although they prioritize work-life balance more aggressively than their older counterparts (Twenge et al., 2010). They value job satisfaction, though this was more evident before the recession, suggesting their work attitudes may be influenced by broader economic contexts rather than inherent generational traits (Kowske et al., 2010). Additionally, this generation brings a notable shift towards less work centrality – prioritizing life outside of work more than previous generations did at the same age. However, they share similar altruistic work values with the older generational groups (Twenge et al., 2010).

Their digital proficiency sets them apart and redefines workplace productivity and problem-solving strategies. Unlike previous generations, Millennials' approach to technology is not just a utility but an integral part of their daily lives, influencing how they engage with tasks and solve problems (Ng et al., 2010). Millennials' interaction with technology distinctly sets them apart from older cohorts. Their upbringing in a digitally connected world has made them exceptionally proficient in leveraging technology for personal and professional use (Hershatter & Epstein, 2010). This comfort with digital tools and platforms impacts their work habits, communication styles, and expectations from the workplace environment.

ATTITUDES OF GENERATIONS ABOUT WORK AND LIFE

Box 5.1 Five Types of Rewards

The evolving workplace landscape not only reflects technological and economic changes but also shifts in the attitudes and values of its occupants. The concepts of rewards in the workplace encompass a variety of factors that motivate and fulfill employees. These rewards can be classified into five main categories: leisure, extrinsic, intrinsic, altruistic, and social rewards.[4] Each type of reward caters to different aspects of human needs and desires in the professional environment.

1   **Leisure:** Leisure rewards refer to the balance between work responsibilities and personal time. This includes the amount of personal or leisure time the job allows, such as flexible working hours, ample vacation time, and policies that support a healthy work-life balance. Employees who perceive an excellent balance between their professional and personal lives will likely be less stressed, more satisfied with their jobs, and more productive.

2   **Extrinsic Rewards:** Extrinsic rewards are tangible rewards externally administered by someone else, typically employers. They include salary, bonuses, benefits, material possessions, promotions, and public recognition. These rewards are essential because they are often seen as a measure of career success and achievement. They can motivate employees to achieve specific goals, improve performance, and provide a sense of security and comfort.

3   **Intrinsic Rewards:** Intrinsic rewards are psychological rewards that individuals reap internally from work. These include feelings of fulfillment, accomplishment, personal growth, and the sense that one's work is meaningful or aligns with personal values and passions. Intrinsic motivation is critical for long-term job satisfaction and engagement. Employees who find their work personally rewarding are more likely to be committed, creative, and enthusiastic about their roles.

4   **Altruistic Rewards:** Altruistic rewards are derived from the ability to contribute to the welfare of others or to make a positive impact on society through one's work. This can include working for non-profit organizations, engaging in corporate social responsibility activities, or simply being in a role that helps people or the environment. For many individuals, the desire to make a difference in the world is a powerful motivator.

5   **Social Rewards:** Social rewards pertain to the benefits derived from interactions and relationships with coworkers, clients, and the broader professional community. This includes camaraderie, friendship, networking opportunities, and belonging to a group or team. Social rewards in the workplace can enhance teamwork, collaboration, and morale and reduce feelings of isolation and alienation.

Shift Towards Valuing Leisure

According to Twenge et al. (2010), there has been a marked increase in the value placed on leisure across the generations. This change is attributed to the social and economic conditions under which the younger generations were raised, particularly Millennials, who grew up observing their parents work extended hours with minimal vacation time (Kupperschmidt, 2000). This has led to a desire for a more balanced approach to work and life. However, it sometimes manifests as a discrepancy between wanting higher pay and status without a proportional commitment to work.

Extrinsic versus Intrinsic Rewards

The research indicates that Millennials emphasize extrinsic rewards, such as pay and prestige, more than Boomers (Twenge et al., 2010). This expectation for higher compensation and a desire for less intensive work schedules indicate a sense of entitlement within this younger cohort. However, the pursuit of altruistic rewards remains consistent across generations, signaling that the motivation to contribute positively to society through work is a universal value. Conversely, interest in social rewards has declined among Millennials, suggesting a shift in how work-related relationships are valued.

Workplace Spirituality and Pride

Mcmurray and Simmers (2019) explored the role of spirituality and religion in the workplace, finding that Generation X and Boomers exhibit higher levels of workplace spirituality and religiosity than Millennials. However, they also noted a generational decline in valuing religion for social reasons.

Smola and Sutton (2002) identified a decline in work pride across all generations from 1974 to 1999, indicating a societal shift towards valuing personal life and individuality over traditional work achievements. Work appeared to take a lower priority in society in the 2000s than the past, and personal value has been less associated with what one does or the effort one puts into work (Smola & Sutton, 2002).

Work Ethic across Generations

Meriac et al. (2010) examined work ethic differences across Boomers, Generation X, and Millennials. They found significant variations, with Boomers displaying a stronger work ethic, particularly believing in the value of hard work and the importance of delaying gratification. This suggests a generational shift in the perception of work and success, with younger generations displaying different attitudes toward the importance and role of work in their lives. Generation X employees exhibited different values than Boomers. The former were found to be less loyal to the company and more oriented toward their sphere. They expected to be promoted more quickly than their older counterparts. They were less likely to feel that work should be an essential part of their lives; however, they correlated one's worth with doing a good job (Smola & Sutton, 2002).

Leadership Preferences of Boomers, Gen X, and Gen Y

Box 5.2 Leadership Preferences of Boomers, Millennials, and Gen X

The leadership preferences of Baby Boomers, Millennials, and Generation X are outlined in Table 5.3. Nevertheless, managers may want to note the following three trends:

1 Older generations appear to prefer extensive picture orientation, while younger generations value a day-to-day focus;
2 Younger generations value a more individually carrying leader; and
3 Generation X individuals expect leaders to earn their respect (Sessa et al., 2007).

Table 5.3 Leadership Values and Preferences of Boomers, Gen X, and Gen Y

Early Boomers	Late Boomers	Early Generation X	Late Generation X	Millennials
Persuasive	Global view	Optimistic	Optimistic	Encouraging
Diplomatic	Dedicated	Persuasive	Experienced	Listens well
Farsighted	Credible	Experienced	Credible	Supportive
Credible	Trusting	Clear focus	Trusting	Trusted
Trusted	Trusted	Participative	Trusted	Dependable
Candid	Dependable	Feedback-oriented	Dependable	Trusting
Honest	Experienced	Credible	Clear focus	Candid
Listens well	Listens well	Trusted	Numerically astute	Honest
Encouraging	Encouraging	Dependable	Perceptive	Focused
	Focused		Feedback-oriented	
	Feedback-oriented			

Source: Adapted from Sessa et al. (2007).

Boomers' Leadership Preferences

Boomers have been traditionally characterized by their strong work ethic, loyalty, and respect for authority (Zemke et al., 1999). In terms of leadership preferences, Boomers tend to value participatory leadership styles. They appreciate leaders who exhibit caring, passion, and honesty, reflecting the transformational leaders of their formative years, such as Mahatma Gandhi and Martin Luther King Jr. (Arsenault, 2004).[5] As a result, they favor environments where leadership is exercised through consensus and collaborative efforts, promoting a sense of unity and shared goals.

For managers, this translates to adopting leadership strategies emphasizing transparency, ethical behavior, and collective decision-making. Encouraging open discussions, recognizing individual contributions, and fostering a team-oriented culture can resonate well with Boomers, enhancing their engagement and productivity.

Generation X's Leadership Preferences

Generation X individuals are often considered independent, resourceful, and self-sufficient (Zemke et al., 1999). They witnessed the rise of technological advancements and corporate downsizing, shaping their skeptical and pragmatic outlook. Unlike their predecessors, Generation X places a high premium on autonomy and egalitarian relationships in the workplace.

This cohort expects leaders to earn their respect and demonstrate competence, embodying the pragmatic and results-oriented leadership exemplified by figures such as Bill Gates (Arsenault, 2004). They prefer leaders who are approachable, flexible, and supportive of work-life balance. Consequently, managers should focus on creating an environment that values meritocracy, provides clear and direct communication, and offers opportunities for professional development. Recognizing the contributions of Generation X employees and providing them with autonomy in their roles can significantly boost their engagement and loyalty.

Generation Y's Leadership Preferences

Millennials have been marked by their affinity for technology, social consciousness, and desire for immediate feedback (Zemke et al., 1999). They grew up in a more nurturing and inclusive environment than previous generations, reflecting their preference for collaborative and transformational leadership styles.

Leadership that emphasizes collaboration, empowerment, and innovation is highly appealing to Generation Y. They thrive under leaders who are not only authoritative but also serve as mentors and coaches. Implementing an adaptive, participative, and feedback-oriented leadership approach can significantly appeal to this cohort's need for personal growth and meaningful work.

CONCLUSIONS

The journey through the intricate landscape of generational cohorts within the workplace – Baby Boomers, Generation X, and Millennials – illuminates diverse perspectives, values, and expectations shaped by distinct formative experiences. This chapter underscores the imperative for leaders to adapt their approaches to resonate with each generation's unique backdrop. By engaging with the comprehensive framework provided, leaders can foster a harmonious and productive workplace that leverages the strengths of each cohort.

By applying Wyatt's (1993) framework, pivotal events, demographic shifts, and societal influences, managers gain a sense of determinants and orientations that sculpt each group's unique worldview. The narrative of the Baby Boomers as pioneers of change, navigating their formative years amidst economic prosperity and social upheaval, paints a picture of a generation driven by idealism and a strong work ethic. The emergence of Generation X, in response to their time's technological and societal shifts, highlights a group marked by independence, pragmatism, and a critical eye toward established norms. Meanwhile, Millennials bring to the forefront an era of digital connectivity, social consciousness, and a reshaped work ethic influenced by their unique upbringing and the global landscape.

Box 5.3 Key Take-Aways for Chapter 5

1   **Step into Their Shoes**: Dive into the historical tapestry that shapes each generation. Understand their unique journeys and perspectives. Viewing your workforce through a generational lens unlocks the secret to seamless communication and deeper connections;

2   **Embrace Generational Strengths**: Leverage the unique assets each cohort brings. Utilize the Boomers' collaborative spirit, Gen X's independent efficiency, and Millennials' innovative and purpose-driven approach to enhance team dynamics and organizational outcomes;

3   **Cultivate Inclusivity**: Welcome each generation's diverse preferences as a source of strength, not a barrier. Integrate these varying expectations into the fabric of your organizational culture and watch as your workplace transforms into a vibrant community where everyone feels valued and heard.

NOTES

1   For an in-depth explanation of the determinants that shape a generational cohort and exemplification of the Baby Boomer cohort, see Wyatt (1993).
2   For a detailed quantitative analysis of similarities and differences in work-related characteristics of Baby Boomers, Generation X, and Generation Y using in-depth indicators, see Tolbize (2008).
3   Lancaster and Stillman (2003) focus on the identifiable characteristics on which the generational groups differ in their worldview of the world of work. See Lancaster and Stillman (2003) for an elaboration on the orientations.
4   In the study conducted by Twenge et al. (2010), the attitudes towards work and life across three generational cohorts—Boomers, Generation X, and Millennials—are dissected to understand these shifts pertaining to leisure, extrinsic, intrinsic, altruistic, and social rewards.
5   See Arsenault (2004) for research on generational groups have leadership preferences that emulate the leaders of their corresponding periods.

REFERENCES

Arsenault, P. (2004). Validating generational differences: A legitimate diversity and leadership issue. *Leadership & Organization Development Journal, 25*(2), 124–141. https://doi.org/10.1108/01437730410521813.

Hershatter, A., & Epstein, M. (2010). Millennials and the world of work: An organization and management perspective. *Journal of Business and Psychology, 25*(2), 211–223. https://doi.org/10.1007/s10869-010-9160-y.

Jennings, A. (2000). Hiring Generation-X. *Journal of Accountancy, 189*, 55. https://www.journalofaccountancy.com/issues/2000/feb/hiringgenerationx.html

Jurkiewicz, C., & Brown, R. (1998). Generational comparisons of public employee motivation. *Review of Public Personnel Administration - Rev Public Pers ADM, 18*(4), 18–37. https://doi.org/10.1177/0734371X9801800403.

Karp, H., Sirias, D., & Arnold, K. (1999). Teams: Why generation X marks the spot - ProQuest. *The Journal for Quality and Participation, 22*(4), 30–33. https://www.proquest.com/docview/219158348?sourcetype=Scholarly%20Journals

Kowske, B. J., Rasch, R., & Wiley, J. (2010). Millennials' (lack of) attitude problem: An empirical examination of generational effects on work attitudes. *Journal of Business and Psychology, 25*(2), 265–279. https://doi.org/10.1007/S10869-010-9171-8.

Kupperschmidt, B. (2000). Multigeneration employees: Strategies for effective management. *The Health Care Manager, 19*(1), 65–76. https://journals.lww.

com/healthcaremanagerjournal/Citation/2000/19010/Multigeneration_Employees__Strategies_for.11.aspx

Lancaster, L. C., & Stillman, D. (2003). *When generations collide: Who they are.* Collins.

Mcmurray, A., & Simmers, C. (2019). The impact of generational diversity on spirituality and religion in the workplace. *Vision: The Journal of Business Perspective, 24*(1), 70–80. https://doi.org/10.1177/0972262919884841.

Meriac, J., Woehr, D., & Banister, C. (2010). Generational differences in work ethic: An examination of measurement equivalence across three cohorts. *Journal of Business Psychology, 25*(2), 315–324. https://doi.org/10.1007/s10869-010-9164-7.

Ng, E. S. W., Schweitzer, L., & Lyons, S. (2010). New generation, great expectations: A field study of the millennial generation. *Journal of Business and Psychology, 25*(2), 281–292. https://www.jstor.org/stable/40605786

O'Bannon, G. (2001). Managing our future: The Generation X factor. *Public Personnel Management, 30*(1), 95–109. https://doi.org/10.1177/009102600103000109.

Ryan, M. (2000). Gerald Celente: He reveals what lies ahead. *Parade Magazine,* September 10, 22–23.

Smola, K., & Sutton, C. (2002). Generational differences: Revisiting generational work values for the new millennium. *Journal of Organizational. Behavior, 23*(SpecIssue), 363–382. https://doi.org/10.1002/job.147.

Staff, J., & Schulenberg, J. (2010). Millennials and the world of work: Experiences in paid work during adolescence. *Journal of Business and Psychology, 25*(2), 247–255. https://doi.org/10.1007/s10869-010-9167-4.

Tolbize, A. (2008). *Generational differences in the workplace.* Research and Training Center on Community Living, University of Minnesota. https://rtc.umn.edu/docs/2_18_Gen_diff_workplace.pdf

Twenge, J., Campbell, S., Hoffman, B., & Lance, C. (2010). Generational differences in work values: Leisure and extrinsic values increasing, social and intrinsic values decreasing. *Journal of Management, 36*(5), 1117–1142. https://doi.org/10.1177/0149206309352524.

Wyatt, D. (1993). *Out of the Sixties.* Cambridge University Press.

Zemke, R., Raines, C., & Filipczak, B. (1999). Generations at work: Managing the clash of Veterans, Boomers. In *Xers, and Nexters in your workplace* (1st ed.). Amacom.

WHO ARE GEN Z-ERS?

Abstract

This chapter delves into the distinctive world of Generation Z, analyzing their unique characteristics, workplace behaviors, and professional expectations against the backdrop of older generations. Growing up at the crossroads of significant technological, global, and socio-economic changes, Generation Z has developed a unique digital fluency and a complex set of values encompassing pragmatism, diversity, and a solid social and environmental conscience. This chapter explores the challenges and opportunities this presents for management, highlighting the need for adaptive workplace strategies that cater to their specific needs for flexibility, meaningful engagement, and personal growth. Furthermore, this chapter emphasizes the importance of understanding Generation Z's unique language and communication styles as crucial for building stronger intergenerational relationships within the workplace.

WHY DOES GENERATION Z POSE SUCH A CONUNDRUM FOR MANAGERS?

Generation Z has grown up in a unique intersection of technological advancement, global connectivity, and socio-economic upheaval. Shaped significantly by the digital age, they have only known a world with the internet, social media, or smartphones, leading to unprecedented tech-savviness and digital fluency. This connectedness has exposed them to diverse perspectives and global issues from a young age, fostering a heightened social awareness and a desire for

DOI: 10.4324/9781032722696-7

authenticity and inclusivity. Economic challenges, such as the aftermath of the 2008 financial crisis, environmental concerns, and a volatile political climate, have instilled in them a sense of pragmatism and a drive for stability and security. Consequently, Gen Z exhibits a blend of entrepreneurial spirit, pragmatic outlook, and solid commitment to social and environmental issues, shaping them into a cohort that values practical action, diversity, and technological innovation in their personal and professional lives.

RESEARCH HIGHLIGHTS

Box 6.1 Research Highlights

The following insights from recent studies shed light on the characteristics and needs of Generation Z in the workplace:

1. According to Twenge (2010), Generation Z finds itself in a unique situation: safer physically yet more exposed emotionally. Their primary interactions occur online rather than face-to-face, leading to a generation that curates its social identity on digital platforms, seeks instant feedback, and typically shies away from conflict. The rise of smartphones, social media, and social justice movements has significantly influenced their worldview yet has left many feeling ill-equipped for traditional employment roles.

2. Generation Z's work environment should adapt to their specific needs. This includes embracing flexible working arrangements, meaningful recognition and rewards, competitive compensation, and opportunities for ongoing feedback.

3. Employment strategies should align with Generation Z's values, integrating human resource practices that foster task performance and emotional investment in the organization. They should also offer substantial learning opportunities and focus on transformative rather than merely transactional work experiences.

4. Managers are crucial in guiding Generation Z employees through realistic job previews, precise expectation setting, thorough onboarding and integration processes, and acknowledging their unique autonomy and meaningful contribution needs.

5. Regular, open communication is essential to addressing Generation Z's concerns, supporting their career development, and promoting their mental health and well-being in the workplace.

Many researchers have been intrigued by the enigma surrounding Generation Z in the workforce. This intrigue stems from their recent entry into the job market, leaving a trail of unanswered questions and curiosity (Bateh, 2019; Mládková, 2017; Parker & Igielnik, 2020; Tapscott, 2009). Bateh (2019) illuminates this area with research suggesting that Generation Z defies a one-size-fits-all leadership style, favoring a more personalized approach that eschews broad categorizations and generalizations.[1]

Twenge (2017) provides insights into the paradoxical nature of Generation Z: they are the most protected generation physically yet navigate an emotional landscape fraught with vulnerabilities. Their social lives unfold more on digital platforms than in physical spaces, shaping a generation that crafts its identity online, craves instant approval, and steers clear of confrontations. The digital tools that define their era – smartphones and social media – and the rise of social justice movements have left them uniquely underprepared for traditional workplace roles (Schroth, 2019).

The work environment that resonates with Generation Z, as identified by (2020), should be dynamic and flexible, incorporating a blend of rewarding practices, feedback mechanisms, and opportunities for personal and professional development. These elements and a commitment to emotional and organizational commitment and transformational tasks create an ideal setting for this emerging workforce.

Managers are, therefore, encouraged to navigate Generation Z's workplace integration with sensitivity and understanding, addressing their distinct needs for autonomy and purpose (Schrotch, 2019). Open and ongoing communication is critical, ensuring that their concerns are heard and their aspirations for career growth and mental well-being are supported (Fernandez et al., 2023).

Furthermore, recent studies by Kuzior et al. (2022) reveal that younger employees, mainly from Generations Y and Z, are seeking more than just a paycheck from their jobs, especially evident during the Great Resignation, driven by a quest for more profound, non-materialistic values. However, what these "meaningful" aspects entail for Generation Z remains unclear for managers.[2]

GEN Z'S WORKPLACE BEHAVIORS

When Generation Z individuals were asked, "What value does work have in your life?" their responses revealed a clear picture of their workplace values. Echoing the findings of Twenge et al. (2010), 60% of these young professionals emphasized the financial rewards of their labor, highlighting a solid drive for extrinsic rewards.[3] Yet, the story extends beyond monetary gains; every member of Generation Z surveyed also demonstrated a profound appreciation for intrinsic rewards, signaling a desire for meaningful development and the pursuit of new experiences that enhance their skill set and personal growth.

The natural similitudes between Generation Z and Millennials become evident in their work preferences. Both groups view job hopping as an integral part of professional life, share an aversion to monotonous tasks, and seek roles that offer more than just a standard workday. They strive for a lifestyle characterized by significant achievements and personal satisfaction, balancing their professional aspirations with a marked emphasis on personal time and leisure.

However, in problem-solving, Generation Z distinguishes itself from older cohorts. Technology is not merely a tool for this group but a fundamental aspect of their approach – instinctive, ever-present, and essential. This tech-savvy generation employs digital solutions effortlessly, addressing challenges with a digital-first strategy that distinguishes them in the contemporary workplace.

Table 6.1 presents the dual perspectives on Generation Z's workplace behaviors: the observations made by managers contrasted with the self-perceptions reported by Generation Z employees.[4] Additionally, Figure 6.1 highlights the juxtaposition of Generation Z's workplace attitudes, showcasing traits such as ambition and desire for quick advancement against a backdrop of reluctance towards consistent effort and traditional commitment. This dichotomy places Generation Z employees in a state of contradiction between their aspirations for immediate achievement and their aversion to the hard grind and routine that often accompany success. These observations align with Twenge et al. (2010), who identified a similar mismatch between expected outcomes and the reality of work effort among Millennials. Amplifying this complex scenario, managers note that Generation Z's lack of experience and a tendency towards defiance

Table 6.1 Gen Z Workplace Behaviors

Category	Participant Group	Summary
Positive workplace behaviors of Gen Z	What their managers say	Young employees have a technological orientation. They have high digital skills and resolve problems through the internet. Their competencies include being clever, educated, and fast learners. They have stamina, are collaborative and interested in expression, and value leisure.
	What Gen Z say	Preferring technology to people, individuals belonging to their generational group have stamina manifested as perseverance, vitality, and a desire to prove themselves. They have a high learning capacity. They desire to express themselves but are collaborative with each other and with other generational groups. They are open-minded, flexible, experimental, and creative and prefer new procedure approaches.
Negative workplace behaviors of Gen Z	What their managers say	The weaknesses of young employees include eagerness, grandiosity, and insubordination. They are aspirants and want immediate success but are also idle. Namely, they are superficial, dislike effort, do not know what they want, and keep changing jobs. Also, they need more experience and, therefore, need ample explanations and are underprepared for the work environment.

(Continued)

Table 6.1 (Continued)

Category	Participant Group	Summary
Negative workplace behaviors of Gen Z	What Gen Z say	Employees of their own generation are idle in the sense that they do not understand the effort, are careless and superficial, lack resistance to stress, dislike routine, and are unstable. Meanwhile, they are entitled, ungrateful, and eager. They want to have it all in a short amount of time. They feel they have choices because their parents support them. The transition from university to the workplace is challenging.

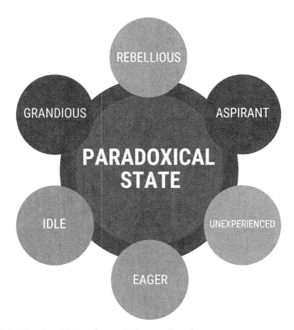

Figure 6.1 The Gen Z Employee Behavior Paradox.

Source: Figure by author.

impede their professional development. This mix of inexperience and a challenge to authority complicates their journey toward achieving tangible outcomes.

A PRIMER ON GEN Z LANGUAGE

For leaders aiming to navigate the evolving landscape of the modern workplace, understanding Generation Z's language is beneficial and essential. This cohort, steeped in the digital era, communicates in a manner that is vastly different from previous generations, as exemplified in Table 6.2. Social media, internet culture, and rapid technological advancement influence their lexicon. By learning Gen Z's language, leaders can bridge communication gaps, foster deeper connections, and enhance team cohesion. It enables leaders to tap into the unique perspectives and innovative ideas that Gen Z brings to the table, thereby fostering an inclusive environment that leverages the full potential of every team member. Moreover, mastering this language signals respect and appreciation for their culture and values, which is crucial for motivating and retaining these young professionals. Understanding Gen Z's language is vital to unlocking their trust, engagement, and loyalty in a dynamic, intergenerational workplace.

Table 6.2 A Primer on Gen Z Language

Gen Z Phrase	Definition	Explanation	Boomer Counterpart
No cap	No lie	A phrase used to emphasize something that is true or accurate.	**No kidding**
Bet	Yes, I agree, or I will do that	A phrase to express agreement or enthusiasm.	**You got it**
Slay	To do something well or impressively	A phrase used to compliment someone's skills or accomplishments.	**Ace**

(Continued)

Table 6.2 (Continued)

Gen Z Phrase	Definition	Explanation	Boomer Counterpart
Tea	Gossip or drama	A phrase used to refer to some interesting or scandalous information.	**The scoop**
Gucci	Good, great, or excellent	A phrase used to express approval or satisfaction.	**A-OK**
Extra	Over the top or excessive	A phrase used to describe something that is flashy, overdone, or unnecessary.	**Too much**
Vibes	The atmosphere or feeling of a place or situation	A phrase used to describe the overall mood or energy of something.	**Feeling**
Deadass	Serious or genuine	A phrase used to emphasize something that is true or sincere.	**For real**
Hit different	To have a strong or unique impact	A phrase used to describe something that is particularly memorable or meaningful.	**Special**
Bussin'	Very good or delicious	A phrase used to express excitement or enjoyment about something, especially food.	**Yummy**
Fire	Excellent or impressive	A phrase used to compliment something or someone's skills.	**Awesome**

CONCLUSIONS

Amidst a backdrop of digital revolution and global shifts, Generation Z has emerged as a cohort marked by technological fluency and a multifaceted approach to life and work. This generation's formative years, influenced by the rapid advancement of the internet, social media, and a landscape of socio-economic fluctuations, have fostered a blend of pragmatism, diversity, and a robust sense of social responsibility.

A compelling insight emerges from the dialogue between Generation Z and their managers, revealing a complex picture of this cohort's workplace demeanor. While managers observe a mix of ambition and reluctance towards traditional work ethics among Generation Z employees, the individuals themselves articulate a demand for meaningful engagement, autonomy, and growth opportunities. This generational narrative is increased by their search for authenticity and inclusivity, alongside a practical action–oriented approach in both personal and professional realms.

Business leaders ought to clarify several pivotal themes: the necessity of tailoring workplace environments to meet the dynamic needs of Generation Z, the importance of transparent and continuous communication, and the imperative to provide realistic job previews and integration strategies that cater to their distinctive blend of values and aspirations.

Box 6.2 Key Take-Aways for Chapter 6

1 **Bridge the Gap with Gen Z Language**: Understanding and utilizing Generation Z's language can significantly enhance communication and connection within the workplace;

2 **Become Digital-First**: Leaders can foster a more inclusive and relatable environment by embracing their digital-first approach and integrating their vernacular;

3 **Prioritize Transparent and Continuous Communication**: Establish open lines of communication to address Generation Z's unique concerns and aspirations.

NOTES

1 Bateh's (2019) mixed-method research on the leadership preferences of Generation Z individuals indicate that "there is no exact leadership standard or profile that this generation admires or follows" (p. 13). Bateh (2019) also predicts that because Generation Z individuals have a disdain for universal-ization and generalization, their preferred leadership style is tailored to the individual.

2 Uncertainty pertaining to Gen Z indicates a pressing need for deeper, qual-itative insights to understand their unique perspectives and workplace dynamics (Aggarwal et al., 2020).

3 30 Gen Z employees responded through an open-ended semi-structured interview.

4 The findings represented in the table are the composite summaries of the open-ended, semi-structured interviews with 30 Gen Z employees and 40 managers belonging to the three older generations. Responses were cod-ified through open and axial coding and transformed into categories using Hycner's (1999) process.

REFERENCES

Aggarwal, A., Sadhna, P., Gupta, S., Mittal, A., & Rastogi, S. (2020). Gen Z entering the workforce: Restructuring HR policies and practices to foster task performance and organizational commitment. *Journal of Public Affairs*, *22*(3), 25–35. https://doi.org/10.1002/pa.2535.

Bateh, D. (2019). Leadership from millennials to Generation Z. *Journal of Advanced Management Science*, *7*(1), 11–14. https://www.joams.com/upload-file/2019/0314/20190314021647211.pdf

Fernandez, J., Lee, J., & Landis, K. (2023). Helping Gen Z employees find their place at work. *Harvard Business Review*. https://hbr.org/2023/01/helping-gen-z-employees-find-their-place-at-work#:~:text=However%2C%20research%20shows%20that%20Gen,and%20earn%20their%20full%20engagement

Hycner, R. H. (1999). Some guidelines for the phenomenological analysis of interview data. In A. Bryman & R. G. Burgess (Eds.), *Qualitative research* (Vol. 3, pp. 143–164). Sage.

Kuzior, A., Kettler, K., & Rąb, Ł. (2022). Great resignation—Ethical, cultural, relational, and personal dimensions of Generation Y and Z employees' engage-ment. *Sustainability*, *14*(11), 6764. https://doi.org/10.3390/su14116764.

Mládková, L. (2017). Learning habits of generation z students. *European Conference of Knowledge Management*, 698–703. https://search.proquest.com/docview/1967756545?accountid=150425

Parker, K., & Igielnik, R. (2020). *On the cusp of adulthood and facing an uncertain future: What we know about Gen Z so far*. Pew Research Center. https://www.pewresearch.org/social-trends/2020/05/14/on-the-cusp-of-adulthood-and-facing-an-uncertain-future-what-we-know-about-gen-z-so-far-2/

Schroth, H. (2019). Are you ready for Gen Z in the workplace? *California Management Review*, *61*(3), 5–18. https://doi.org/10.1177/0008125619841006.

Tapscott, D. (2009). *Grown up digital: How the net generation is changing your world* (1st ed.). Mcgraw-Hill.

Twenge, J. M. (2010). A review of the empirical evidence on generational differences in work attitudes. *Journal of Business Psychology*, *25*, 201–210. https://doi.org/10.1007/Sl0869-010-9165-6.

Twenge, J., S. Campbell, B. Hoffman, and C. Lance. 2010. Generational differences in work values: Leisure and extrinsic values increasing, social and intrinsic values decreasing. *Journal of Management, 36*(5), 1117–1142. doi: 10.1177/0149206309352246.

Twenge, J. 2017. *IGen: Why Today's Super-Connected Kids Are Growing up Less Rebellious, More Tolerant, Less Happy, and Completely Unprepared for Adulthood*. Atria Books.

PART II

HANDS-ON
LEADERSHIP – ACTIONABLE
STRATEGIES FOR GEN Z INTEGRATION

WHAT ARE GEN Z-ERS' WORKPLACE EXPECTATIONS AND WORK ETHIC VALUES?

Abstract

This chapter delves into Gen Z's Job Crisis Loop, exploring their career choices and the factors contributing to high turnover. It proposes essential knowledge to address these challenges and engage Gen Z talent effectively. It highlights Generation Z's predilection for workplaces that combine high financial compensation with strong social interactions and a supportive culture, marking a significant shift from the priorities of previous generations. Young employees frequently change jobs due to unmet expectations, which creates a cyclical pattern identified as the Job Crisis Loop. This chapter further describes Generation Z's demand for work-life balance, their aspirations for rapid progression and acknowledgment, and their requirement for an empowering and engaging work environment.

In the dynamically evolving workplace landscape, understanding Generation Z's work expectations, preferences, and leadership ideals is paramount for contemporary business leaders. This chapter delves into Generation Z's intricate profile, identifying their distinct needs and values as they navigate various life stages and integrate into the work environment.

Highlighting Generation Z's passion for development, desire for a balanced workday, and unique blend of extrinsic and intrinsic motivational factors, the analysis provides a comprehensive view of Generation Z's ideal workplace and the attributes they seek in leaders. Table 7.1 exhibits Gen Z's prevalent answers to managers' pressing questions.[1]

DOI: 10.4324/9781032722696-9

Table 7.1 Workplace Preferences of Gen Z

Category	*Gen Z Responses*
Value of work	Work is important and has financial value. It also allows one to acquire experience and develop oneself. Work fulfills a social aspect and is valuable to society. Work-life balance is essential.
Ideal workplace	High financial compensation and recognition are most important. Also, work should be enjoyable. The workplace should be a place for innovation with transparency, a positive attitude, and collegiality. The following are preferred regarding the schedule and workload: an eight-hour program, schedule flexibility and no-shift working, a clear work plan, feedback, and little stress.
Mentors/heroes	The main heroes or mentors are entertainers who can be artists, influencers, athletes, or one's parents. They can also be experts, IT business leaders, more experienced professionals, or educators.
Admired qualities of leaders	A leader must be a good communicator, supportive, and understanding; know how to motivate employees; and have teaching capabilities. A leader should be technology-oriented, competent in terms of goal-attainment, planning, and overall management, and firm but calm and positive. A leader should be an example, sincere, and approachable; work alongside employees; and consider the employee perspective.
Expected workplace recompenses	The primary workplace recompenses are financial rewards and praise. Feedback, a positive relationship with coworkers and the manager, flexible working hours, and educational resources are also expected.

WORK EXPECTATIONS AND PREFERENCES OF GENERATION Z

Understanding each generation's diverse needs and preferences is crucial for creating engaging and productive work environments as the workforce evolves. For Generation Z – those at the early stages of their career trajectory – personal development and acquiring new experiences are paramount. These needs reflect their life stage and their integration into a multigenerational workforce.

THE IDEAL WORKPLACE FOR GENERATION Z

This cohort envisions an ideal workplace that balances a traditional eight-hour workday with the flexibility to adapt their schedule to fit their lifestyle. Unlike Millennials, Generation Z places a higher value on social benefits, with 77% highlighting the importance of cowork-ers and a sense of belonging (Twenge, 2010). They seek a workplace that offers financial compensation and recognition – the top extrinsic rewards – and fosters intrinsic, leisure, and social rewards, underlin-ing a shift from previous generations' preferences.

LEADERSHIP QUALITIES VALUED BY GENERATION Z

The leadership preferences of Generation Z reflect a blend of past ideals and contemporary realities. This generation values collabora-tive, competent, and transparent leadership, emphasizing technolog-ical savviness, a trait that previous generations should have prioritized. Generational groups progressed from a directive preference for Bommers to a coach preference for Generation X and a partner preference for Millenials (Lancaster & Stillman, 2002). They seek leaders who are not only directive and able to provide clear guidance but also embody the qualities of a mentor or coach. This indicates a return to more structured leadership from the more laissez-faire style preferred by Millennials, likely a response to Generation Z's relative inexperience in the workforce.

WORKPLACE REWARDS AND COMPENSATION FOR GENERATION Z

Regarding workplace rewards, Generation Z strongly prefers extrin-sic rewards, particularly financial benefits, praise, and recognition (Twenge et al., 2010). The desire for acclaim is just as crucial as the need for money. This inclination towards external validation and financial incentives mirrors a broader societal shift towards more materialistic values. However, employers should aim to balance these extrinsic rewards with opportunities for intrinsic rewards and foster a supportive and inclusive workplace culture.

MENTORS AND HEROES: SHAPING THE EXPECTATIONS OF GENERATION Z

The influences on Generation Z extend beyond the workplace, shaping their expectations and professional aspirations. Parents, entertainers, and IT professionals, particularly those recognized as industry leaders, serve as key figures for this generation. These mentors and heroes shape Generation Z's self-concept, professional aspirations, and expectations from their work environment and leaders. These three categories are treated below in more depth:

IT Business Leaders: For instance, the admiration for IT leaders reflects Generation Z's inherent technological orientation, influencing their expectations for digital competency in their workplace leaders. The admiration for IT business leaders remained steady from Gen X onward, even though critical figures may have changed from Bill Gates to Elon Musk.

Influencers: Generation Z's admiration for influencers marks a shift in the archetypal figures admired by young professionals. Similar to earlier generations' fascination with celebrities, this group gravitates toward social media influencers – modern-day microcelebrities whose authenticity and relatability seem to surpass traditional fame (Khamis et al., 2016; Senft, 2013). This inclination towards influencers reflects broader aspirations among Generation Z to achieve similar recognition, often viewing this status as an attainable part-time role (Tolani & Sao, 2020). However, this admiration may skew their workplace expectations, leading to a clash between the grandiose perceptions fueled by social media and the realities of professional environments (van Driel & Dumitrica, 2021). For business leaders, understanding this gap is crucial; Generation Z enters the workforce with a set of expectations shaped by digital culture, which may require recalibration to align with actual workplace dynamics.

Parents: Gen Z employees from nuclear families view their parents as heroes and mentors (Mihai & Butiu, 2012). This parental influence is instrumental in shaping the adult identities of Generation

Z through various mechanisms[2] (Musick & Bumpass, 1999). Consequently, when Generation Z employees enter the workforce, they bring a well-defined self-concept cultivated by their parents' guidance. Individuals tend to act in ways that affirm their self-views and gravitate towards others who reinforce these perceptions, maintaining their engagement as long as their sense of self is affirmed (Scroggins, 2008). Engagement fluctuates when managers treat employees as their parents may have told them they should not be treated.

JOB CRISES LOOP: WHY YOUNG EMPLOYEES LEAVE JOBS

Box 7.1 Job Crises Loop In Brief

Young employees reach the workplace with unrealistic expectations – often due to the influencer culture that models a life of fast achievement. Young recruits desire fast rewards in the form of pay and generous praise. Tenured employees expect young ones to demonstrate consistent effort over time – an idea that baffles recruits and makes them think they are oppressed in the workplace.

For young employees, the internal conflict in the workplace is between distinction and discretionary effort, usually perceived in the short and long term. Resolving this dilemma results in the employee developing resiliency, culminating in understanding timing, and gaining a sense of place. Young employees will be in a loop if the crises are not resolved.

The Job Crises Loop exhibits the perpetual consequences of not resolving the distinction vs. effort internal conflict. Young employees face this conflict at every new job. The employee needs to resolve the dispute, gain prestige and power, and, in the hope of receiving distinction in the short term without long-term discretionary effort, change jobs. Upon getting to the new job, the young employee attempts to eschew the conflict by changing jobs once more.

The journey through the workplace can often feel like a clash between dreams and reality, particularly for younger employees. The disjunction between expected and actual workplace experiences, especially among younger employees, has become a significant driver of employee disengagement. This phenomenon underscores a universal truth: the realities of professional life seldom align with one's idealized vision, and people with unattained dreams tend to engage more in behaviors that can be perceived as unfavorable (Schweitzer et al., 2004). This disparity, particularly pronounced in the Millennial cohort, leads to a pervasive disillusionment (Kupperschmidt, 2000; Lancaster & Stillman, 2003; Twenge, 2010). Millennials, followed closely by Generation Z, enter the workplace armed with lofty expectations, only to confront a reality that falls short, breeding a cycle of disengagement.

As seen in Chapter 6, a consensus emerged between managers and Gen Z-ers portraying Generation Z employees as collaborative, intelligent, and technologically adept. However, there is a noted disparity in expectations. While praised for their enthusiasm and innovation, Generation Z is also perceived as overambitious and occasionally disengaged, with managers pointing out their inexperience and preference for leisure over labor. Considering their workplace behaviors and the disparity with their workplace preferences, Gen Z-ers face an internal crisis.

Box 7.2 Boomers' Workplace Dilemma

Generational cohorts encounter unique internal challenges influenced by their specific generational attributes and organizational roles. Baby Boomers, for instance, confront a critical choice: to share their valuable knowledge, thereby nurturing organizational growth and intergenerational cohesion, or to retain this wisdom, risking isolation and a breakdown in knowledge continuity. They are caught in a legacy dilemma – whether to impart their accumulated wisdom to succeeding generations or to hold back a decision that dictates their sense of contribution and, consequently, their workplace satisfaction.

This friction can be contextualized within the framework of Erikson's (1982) theory of psychosocial stages,[3] which posits that each generation faces distinct internal conflicts shaped by its unique societal roles and stages in life.

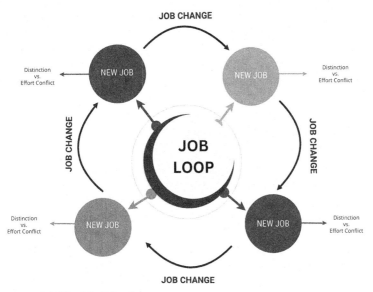

Figure 7.1 The Job Crises Loop.

Source: Figure by author.

Contrastingly to Boomers, the dilemma for Generation Z is characterized by a tension between the pursuit of immediate acknowledgment versus the commitment to sustained effort. This internal conflict encapsulates the quintessence of Erickson's theory, where resolving such crises is essential for developmental progress. Success in this arena enables Generation Z employees to develop resilience and a nuanced understanding of their professional trajectory. However, failure to reconcile these opposing forces thrusts them into a recurring Job Crises Loop – illustrated in Figure 7.1.

The Job Crises Loop, as depicted, signifies the relentless cycle faced by individuals unable to balance the quest for quick validation with the realities of long-term career development. This pattern of job hopping, driven by unmet expectations for rapid advancement and recognition, leads to repetitive challenges, inhibiting personal growth and professional stability.

Leaders and HR professionals must recognize and address these generational dynamics. Developing a nuanced understanding of these internal conflicts and crafting strategies to bridge expectation gaps can lead to more engaged, productive, and harmoniously integrated workplace environments. This approach mitigates the risk of the Job Crises Loop and aligns organizational objectives with the diverse aspirations of today's multigenerational workforce.

CONCLUSIONS

In the rapidly evolving landscape of today's workplace, leaders and managers must grasp the unique challenges and expectations Generation Z faces to foster a more engaging and productive environment. This demographic seeks a blend of traditional and modern work values: they prioritize personal development and new experiences while craving a balanced workday, highlighting a departure from previous generations with an emphasis on financial and social rewards. However, the gap between their expectations, influenced significantly by social media and the digital age, and workplace realities can lead to disconnection and disengagement, notably reflected in the Job Crisis Loop phenomenon. As they navigate their career path, Gen Z employees are caught in a cycle of seeking immediate recognition without the corresponding long-term effort, leading to repeated job changes and unmet expectations.

Leaders must, therefore, adapt their approaches to meet the nuanced needs of this new generation. Understanding that Gen Z values transparent, collaborative, and technologically adept leadership can help bridge the gap between generational expectations and workplace realities. By fostering a culture that aligns with these values, leaders can encourage Gen Z employees to develop resilience and a deeper understanding of their professional trajectory. This shift requires a move away from purely directive leadership and towards a model that offers straightforward guidance while also serving as a mentor and coach, aiding in resolving the internal conflict between the desire for instant gratification and the realities of sustained effort.

To mitigate the challenges presented by the Job Crisis Loop and align organizational objectives with the aspirations of Generation Z, leaders must cultivate workplace environments that offer balanced rewards and acknowledge the changing dynamics of work-life expectations. By providing opportunities for intrinsic rewards and fostering a supportive culture, organizations can enhance engagement among Generation Z employees. Leaders and HR professionals should focus on developing strategies that recognize this generation's unique contributions and provide them with the tools and support needed to navigate the complexities of the modern workplace. This approach will address the generational dynamics and contribute to a more integrated and productive organizational environment.

Box 7.3 Key Take-Aways for Chapter 7

1 **Recognize and Reward**: Acknowledge the contributions of Generation Z employees regularly. While financial incentives are necessary, do not underestimate the power of praise and recognition in building their loyalty and satisfaction;

2 **Bridge the Expectation-Reality Gap**: Be proactive in understanding and managing Gen Z workers' expectations. Address the disconnect between their ideal workplace and workplace environment to prevent disillusionment and disengagement;

3 **Understand Their Influencers**: Recognize the impact of external influences on Generation Z's expectations and aspirations, leverage this understanding to enhance engagement and retention strategies, and understand their influencers.

NOTES

1 The findings represented in the table are the composite summaries of the open-ended, semi-structured interviews with 30 Gen Z employees. Responses were codified through open and axial coding and transformed into categories using Hycner's (1999) process.

2 The phenomenon reaches beyond the current work. See Musick and Bumpass (1999).

3 The theory outlines eight stages of psychosocial development from infancy to late adulthood. At each stage, individuals face a conflict between two

opposing states that shapes personality. Successfully resolving conflicts leads to virtues like hope, will, purpose, and integrity. See Erikson (1982) for the full explanation of the phenomenon.

REFERENCES

Erikson, E. H. (1982). *The life cycle completed: A review.* Norton.

Khamis, S., Ang, L., & Welling, R. (2016). Self-branding, 'micro-celebrity,' and the rise of social media influencers. *Celebrity Studies, 8*(2), 1–18. https://doi.org/10.1080/19392397.2016.1218292.

Kupperschmidt, B. (2000). Multigeneration employees: Strategies for effective management. *The Health Care Manager, 19*(1), 65–76. https://journals.lww.com/healthcaremanagerjournal/Citation/2000/19010/Multigeneration_Employees__Strategies_for.11.aspx

Lancaster, L. C., & Stillman, D. (2003). *When generations collide: Who they are.* Collins.

Mihai, A., & Butiu, O. (2012). The family in Romania: Cultural and economic context and implications for treatment. *International Review of Psychiatry, 24*(2), 139–143. https://doi.org/10.3109/09540261.2012.658029.

Musick, K., & Bumpass, L. (1999). How do prior experiences in the family affect transitions to adulthood. In A. Booth, A. C. Crouter, & M. Shanahan (Eds.), *Transitions to Adulthood in a Changing Economy: No Work, Family: No Future* (69–102). Westport, CT: Praeger.

Schweitzer, M., Ordóñez, L., & Douma, B. (2004). Goal setting as a motivator of unethical behavior. *Academy of Management Journal, 47*, 422–432. https://doi.org/10.2307/20159591.

Scroggins, W. A. (2008). The relationship between employee fit perceptions, job performance, and retention: Implications of perceived fit. *Employee Responsibilities and Rights Journal, 20*(1), 57–71. https://doi.org/10.1007/s10672-007-9060-0.

Senft, T. M. (2013). *Microcelebrity and the branded self* (J. Hartley, J. Burgess, & A. Bruns, Eds.). Wiley-Blackwell.

Tolani, K. C., & Sao, R. (2020). Influence of micro-celebrities on Generation Z: Perception, customer engagement, and career option. In A. Shrivastava, G. Jain, & J. Paul (Eds.), *Circular economy and re-commerce in the fashion industry* (pp. 54–72). IGI Global. https://doi:10

Twenge, J. M. (2010). A review of the empirical evidence on generational differences in work attitudes. *Journal of Business Psychology*, *25*, 201–210. https://doi.org/10.1007/Sl0869-010-9165-6.

van Driel, L., & Dumitrica, D. (2021). Selling brands while staying "Authentic": The professionalization of Instagram influencers. *Convergence*, *27*(1), 66–84. https://doi.org/10.1177/1354856520902136.

HOW TO ATTRACT GEN Z EMPLOYEES IN THE WORKPLACE

Abstract

Focusing on employer branding, this chapter guides readers on strategies to attract Gen Z talent. It highlights common pitfalls in employer branding that may deter this cohort, offering practical solutions to build an appealing workplace culture. Additionally, this chapter discusses the strategic implementation of employer branding, emphasizing the alignment of an organization's values, people strategy, and HR policies to engage the right talent effectively. Through a comparative case study and a series of checklists, this chapter guides leaders in crafting a workplace that resonates with Generation Z's dynamic and evolving expectations, ultimately positioning organizations to thrive in an era of rapid workforce turnover.

Leaders aiming to attract Gen Z talent may want to implement a strategic employer brand that resonates with this generation's values and leverage digital platforms. In reading the previous chapter, executives may have realized that Generation Z, a considerable segment of the current workforce, has distinct values and expectations different from previous generations. To attract these young talents, organizations must adapt their employer branding to align with Gen Z's priorities, such as equitable pay, benefits, social justice, work–life balance, and opportunities for learning and growth (Fernandez et al., 2023). This demographic seeks authenticity and transparency from potential employers, prioritizing companies that reflect their values and offer a culture of inclusivity and development (Schroth, 2019).

DOI: 10.4324/9781032722696-10

Moreover, a company's digital presence and stance on social issues heavily influence Gen Z's approach to job selection. They utilize online platforms to gauge an employer's brand and ethos, making it essential for companies to manage their online reputation proactively and to leverage social media effectively. Given their digital nativity, a positive online employer brand is crucial to attract Gen Z candidates.

Furthermore, this generation's inclination towards social responsibility means they are drawn to companies with a solid commitment to community impact. Emphasizing a company's social initiatives can significantly boost its attractiveness to Gen Z candidates.

A NOTE ON EMPLOYER BRANDING

An employer brand reflects how a company markets itself to potential and current employees, highlighting what makes it unique and desirable as a place to work.[1] This brand strategy includes the set of attributes and qualities, often intangible, that define an organization's distinctiveness, promise a specific kind of employment experience, and appeal to those who will thrive and perform best in its culture (Highhouse et al., 2009). There are variations between word of mouth, reputation, and image indicators, yet these elements should not concern managers at this stage (Lievens & Slaughter, 2016). A well-crafted employer brand connects an organization's values, people strategy, and HR policies and should be consistently integrated throughout the company's approach to people management. This alignment ideally extends beyond mere rhetoric, reflecting the real experiences of employees.

Employer branding for Gen Z is essential for several reasons. It helps organizations attract, recruit, retain, and engage the right people. By establishing a strong employer brand, companies can compete more effectively for top talent and enhance their credibility (Slaughter et al., 2004). This becomes particularly significant when facing recruitment challenges – as most companies presently do – as a positive employer brand can significantly impact performance by retaining talent and boosting levels of employee engagement (Cable & Turban, 2003). Businesses can gain competitive advantages and safeguard their brand image by strategically managing how the organization is perceived as an employer (Dineen & Williamson, 2012).

Box 8.1 Employer Brand Audit Checklist

This Audit is not merely an exercise in checking boxes; it is a strategic journey toward understanding the pulse of the newest generation in the workforce, thereby sculpting a workplace that is attractive and supportive of their growth and professional aspirations.

Corporate Image and Values

☐ **Social Responsibility**: Evaluate your organization's commitment to social issues important to Gen Z, such as sustainability, diversity, and inclusion. Is this commitment visible and tangible – such as through a CSR report?

☐ **Innovation**: Determine if your company is perceived as innovative. Does your brand communicate a forward-thinking mindset and embrace new technologies?

Work Environment and Culture

☐ **Flexibility**: Check if your work policies accommodate flexible schedules, remote working options, and work-life balance, crucial factors for Gen Z. Are Gen Z-ers offered, for instance, mental health days?

☐ **Inclusive Culture**: How diverse is your workplace? Are there policies and programs that promote equality and inclusivity?

☐ **Growth and Development**: Is there clear communication about career pathways and upskilling programs?

Communication and Engagement

☐ **Digital Presence**: Evaluate your online presence across platforms preferred by Gen Z? Is your content engaging and relatable to the younger audience?

☐ **Feedback Mechanisms**: Examine the effectiveness of your feedback channels. Are there mechanisms for Gen Z employees to voice their opinions and contribute to decision-making?

☐ **Community Engagement**: Determine the extent of your organization's involvement in community and social causes. Does your brand actively participate in initiatives that resonate with Gen Z values?

Recruitment and Onboarding

☐ **Recruitment Strategies:** Do job descriptions and adverts reflect job roles?

☐ **Onboarding Experience:** Assess the effectiveness of your onboarding process. Is it engaging, informative, and on-demand?

☐ **Internship and Apprenticeship Programs:** Are development programs in place? Are they designed to provide a meaningful, hands-on experience?

Compensation and Benefits

☐ **Competitive Analysis:** Compare your compensation packages with industry standards and Gen Z expectations. Are your salary, benefits, and perks competitive?

☐ **Well-being Programs:** Assess the availability and accessibility of mental health and well-being programs. Are these programs communicated and encouraged among employees?

☐ **Unique Benefits:** Identify any unique benefits your company offers that are particularly attractive to Gen Z, such as student loan assistance or technology stipends.

Engaging with this audit is a step towards bridging the gap between traditional workplace norms and Generation Z's dynamic, evolving expectations.

BOMMER VS GEN Z EMPLOYER BRANDING: A CASE STUDY

ClassicCorp's strategic pivot compellingly juxtaposes embracing both ends of the generational spectrum – the Baby Boomers and Generation Z.[2] This comparative analysis delves into how a traditional manufacturing giant, ClassicCorp, adeptly rebranded to attract distinct age cohorts.

Revitalizing Tradition for Baby Boomers: ClassicCorp's initial challenge lay in rejuvenating its appeal to Baby Boomer professionals, a demographic characterized by their quest for stability, respect for experience, and preference for clear organizational structures. The firm's strategic overhaul concentrated on accentuating long-term job security, honoring the wisdom of age through a Legacy Mentorship Program, and adapting to the life-stage needs of Boomers with flexible work arrangements and enhanced health care benefits. These initiatives were amplified through platforms like LinkedIn, resonating with the Boomer demographic.

Navigating New Horizons for Generation Z: In contrast, Classic-Corp's – rebranded Corp Z – pivot towards Generation Z required an altogether different strategy, reflecting the priorities of a younger, digital-first generation seeking purpose, innovation, and flexibility. This shift saw the company embedding sustainability and social responsibility into its DNA, revamping its digital communication to align with Gen Z's platforms of choice, such as Instagram and Tik-Tok, and introducing comprehensive development programs catering to its growth aspirations. Implementing flexible working arrangements and a strong emphasis on mental health days resonated deeply with Gen Z values, resulting in a significant boost in applications from this cohort.

The dual strategy underscores the importance of multifaceted, inclusive employer branding that resonates across age groups, ultimately enriching the organization's culture and driving innovative outcomes from a diverse talent pool.

BUILD A GEN Z-CENTRIC EMPLOYER BRAND

Leaders should spearhead the integration of cutting-edge technology across all business dimensions, ensuring the company's online presence mirrors a technologically proficient and future-oriented workplace. Strategic utilization of platforms such as LinkedIn, Instagram, and TikTok to portray the organization's culture and ethos is essential. Content that underscores innovation, teamwork, and societal contributions will magnetize Generation Z's attention. Furthermore, refining the company's online career portal to ensure it is mobile-responsive, intuitive, and seamless accentuates a commitment to modernity and efficiency, aligning with the expectations of digital natives.

Transparency and authenticity rank high on Generation Z's list of prerequisites for potential employers. This demographic demands a genuine peek into the life within a company, coupled with a firm stance on pivotal issues like diversity and environmental sustainability. Involve Gen Z staff in crafting authentic narratives and testimonials, thereby forging a genuine connection with prospective employees. Articulating the organization's social responsibility initiatives and illustrating tangible achievements in these realms can significantly enhance trust and resonance among this cohort. Additionally, the personal branding of managers emerges as an integral element of the broader corporate brand, especially poignant in attracting Gen Z professionals. Leaders are expected to be more than mere figureheads; they must be relatable, transparent, and socially aware. Engaging actively on social media and sharing professional milestones and personal insights can strip away the corporate veneer, presenting a relatable and compelling figure to Gen Z job seekers.

Box 8.2 Build a Gen Z-Centric Employer Brand: Checklist

- [ ] **Conduct a Digital Audit**: Evaluate your company's digital footprint from the perspective of a Gen Z job seeker. Ensure your website, social media profiles, and job postings are updated and mobile-friendly, and use Gen Z language.
- [ ] **Showcase Technological Savvy**: Highlight your company's use of technology in recruits' education, daily operations, project management, and communication tools.
- [ ] **Enhance Online Visibility**: Develop an engaging online presence on platforms popular with Gen Z, such as Instagram, LinkedIn, and TikTok. Share behind-the-scenes content, employee stories, and initiatives your company is passionate about.
- [ ] **Promote Diversity and Inclusion**: Share your diversity, equity, and inclusion goals and achievements publicly. Include statistics, ongoing programs, and employee testimonials.
- [ ] **Emphasize Sustainability and Social Responsibility**: Outline your sustainability efforts and community involvement.
- [ ] **Foster Transparency and Authenticity**: Create content that gives a realistic view of your workplace. Use actual employees rather than actors in your employer branding materials and allow them to share their genuine experiences and challenges.

CONCLUSIONS

A paradigm shift in employer branding is essential to attract Generation Z to the workplace. Organizations may want to mold their employer brands to mirror Generation Z's unique expectations and values, focusing on creating a tech-forward, inclusive, and socially responsible work environment. A digital-first approach, showcasing innovation, and maintaining a solid online presence is no longer optional but mandatory to captivate this digitally native cohort.

The role of personal branding for leadership in shaping the employer brand can no longer take a backseat. This alignment between personal leadership and employer brands can significantly boost a company's attractiveness to Generation Z, fostering a workplace that draws in this new wave of talent and supports their professional growth and aspirations. Ultimately, engaging with these strategies marks a step towards bridging the gap between traditional workplace norms and Generation Z's dynamic, evolving expectations, and positioning organizations to thrive in an era of rapid turnover.

Box 8.3 Key Take-Aways for Chapter 8

1 **Adopt a Digital-First Approach:** To resonate with tech-savvy Generation Z, embrace and integrate cutting-edge technology across all facets of the business. A robust online presence on platforms like LinkedIn, Instagram, and TikTok, showcasing the company's innovative and collaborative culture, is crucial to attract this cohort's attention;

2 **Brand Leaders:** Encourage managers to develop their brands to be more relatable, transparent, and digitally savvy. Their genuine engagement on social platforms can humanize the corporate brand, making it more appealing to Gen Z individuals seeking accessible and authentic leadership;

3 **Promote a Gen Z-Friendly Company:** Demonstrate, through actions and policies, that your company is aligned with Gen Z values such as inclusivity, social responsibility, and technological advancement. Active promotion of these attributes, leveraging Gen Z employees as brand ambassadors, can significantly enhance the organization's attractiveness to this generation.

NOTES

1   Further differentiations between internal brands and external brands engage with the umbrella term of brand systems, necessitating ample discussion that will not be treated in this chapter. For a detailed discussion on employer branding, employer image dimensions, and measurement, see Lievens and Slaughter (2016).
2   The case study uses a fictional name to maintain confidentiality.

REFERENCES

Cable, D. M., & Turban, D. B. (2003). The value of organizational reputation in the recruitment context: A brand-equity perspective. *Journal of Applied Social Psychology*, *33*(11), 2244–2266. https://doi.org/10.1111/j.1559-1816.2003.tb01883.x.

Dineen, B. R., & Williamson, I. O. (2012). Screening-oriented recruitment messages: Antecedents and relationships with applicant pool quality. *Human Resource Management*, *51*(3), 343–360. https://doi.org/10.1002/hrm.21476.

Fernandez, J., Lee, J., & Landis, K. (2023). Helping Gen Z employees find their place at work. *Harvard Business Review*. https://hbr.org/2023/01/helping-gen-z-employees-find-their-place-at-work#:~:text=However%2C%20research%20shows%20that%20Gen,and%20earn%20their%20full%20engagement

Highhouse, S., Brooks, M. E., & Gregarus, G. (2009). An organizational impression management perspective on the formation of corporate reputations. *Journal of Management*, *35*(6), 1481–1493. https://doi.org/10.1177/0149206309348788.

Lievens, F., & Slaughter, J. E. (2016). Employer image and employer branding: What we know and what we need to know. *Annual Review of Organizational Psychology and Organizational Behavior*, *3*(Volume 3), 407–440. https://doi.org/10.1146/annurev-orgpsych-041015-062501.

Schroth, H. (2019). Are you ready for Gen Z in the workplace? *California Management Review*, *61*(3), 5–18. https://doi.org/10.1177/0008125619841006.

Slaughter, J. E., Zickar, M. J., Highhouse, S., & Mohr, D. C. (2004). Personality trait inferences about organizations: Development of a measure and assessment of construct validity. *Journal of Applied Psychology*, *89*(1), 85–103. https://doi.org/10.1037/0021-9010.89.1.85.

HOW TO REDESIGN JOB DESCRIPTIONS FOR GEN Z-ERS

Abstract

This chapter addresses how job descriptions and roles can be tailored to meet Gen Z's preferences and skills. It emphasizes the strategic role of job advertisements as tools for conveying information and as pivotal assets in attracting talent. With a focus on aligning job descriptions with the preferences and skills of Gen Z – characterized by their quest for flexibility, digital savviness, and social consciousness – this chapter provides a comprehensive audit framework for evaluating and refining job descriptions. This chapter offers actionable insights for business leaders, executives, and managers to engage Gen Z talent through a comparative analysis of generational preferences in job descriptions.

The strategic role of job advertisements in the early stages of recruitment cannot be overstated, a conclusion well-supported by a robust body of empirical research.[1]

The design and content of job ads have been shown to critically influence several key recruitment outcomes, including how potential employees perceive the attractiveness of an organization (Avery, 2003), the overall image of the organization (Gatewood et al., 1993; Highhouse et al., 2009), the likelihood of a job seeker (Reeve & Schultz, 2004), and the perceived credibility of the information (Allen et al., 2004; Thorsteinson & Highhouse, 2003; Walker et al., 2009).

Moreover, the capacity for organizations to tailor job advertisements to attract applications from the most suitable candidates has

DOI: 10.4324/9781032722696-11

been well documented (Avery, 2003; Brown et al., 2006; James et al., 2001; Walker et al., 2007). This suggests a compelling opportunity for managers and executives to shape their recruitment strategies proactively through thoughtful job ad creation.

For organizations, the implications are clear: Job advertisements are not just informational tools but strategic assets that can significantly influence the fit of applicants (Dineen & Soltis, 2011). By prioritizing clarity, appeal, and strategic messaging within job ads, leaders can effectively guide recruitment outcomes in favor of the organization and its prospective Gen Z employees.

Box 9.1 Gen Z Job Description Audit

Creating an audit for your company's job descriptions can help ensure they resonate with this Gen Z demographic and align with their language and comprehension levels.

Company Overview and Values

☐ Does the company overview highlight innovation, diversity, and social responsibility?

☐ Are the company's core values clearly stated and aligned with Gen Z interests such as sustainability, equality, and community involvement?

Job Title and Summary

☐ Is the job title modern and reflective of the role's responsibilities and level?

☐ Does the job summary engage the reader by explaining the impact of the role and its importance within the company and at a more significant societal level?

Flexibility and Work-Life Balance

☐ Is there a mention of flexible working hours or remote work opportunities?

☐ Are work-life balance benefits such as mental health days, wellness programs, or flexible PTO policies highlighted?

Professional Development

- ☐ Does the description include opportunities for professional growth, such as mentorship, training programs, or access to learning resources?
- ☐ Are there clear pathways for advancement or role progression outlined?

Technology and Innovation

- ☐ Is there evidence that the company is technologically advanced or innovative?
- ☐ Are the tools and technologies such as AI used in the role modern and relevant?

Diversity and Inclusion

- ☐ Is there a clear statement promoting diversity and inclusion within the company?
- ☐ Are there examples or initiatives mentioned that support these claims?

Compensation and Benefits

- ☐ Are the salary range and benefits clearly outlined?
- ☐ Do the benefits meet the needs and interests of Gen Z, such as health insurance, mental health support, and environmental initiatives?

Responsibilities and Requirements

- ☐ Are the responsibilities listed in a Gen Z language-friendly manner?
- ☐ Are the requirements realistic, specific, measurable, and not overly demanding for entry-level positions?

Application Process

- ☐ Is the application process straightforward to understand?
- ☐ Are there inclusive statements encouraging diverse applicants to apply?
- ☐ Is the application process through an online platform?

Modern Language and Tone

☐ Is the job description written in a modern, relatable tone without excessive jargon?
☐ Does it speak directly to Gen Z candidates and their career aspirations?
☐ Is the job promoted in Gen Z hubs?

Feedback and Revision

☐ Is there a system for receiving feedback on job descriptions from Gen Z employees?
☐ Are there regular reviews and updates to ensure the job description remains relevant and engaging?

JOB DESCRIPTIONS TO TARGET GEN Z-ERS

The following description appeals to Gen Z values such as flexibility, creativity, social justice, and digital savviness. It emphasizes a collaborative and dynamic work culture, opportunities for personal growth, and a commitment to diversity and inclusion. Most importantly, it is written in Gen Z language: words are simplified and little jargon, and contents are listed.

Title: Digital Content Creator
Location: Flexible / Remote / Anywhere with Internet Access
About Us: At InnovateTech,[2] we are not just a tech company; we are a movement towards a more connected, sustainable, and innovative future. Our platforms empower voices worldwide, making technology accessible and enjoyable. We seek a Social Media and Digital Engagement Coordinator ready to dive into the digital world, spark conversations, and drive our mission forward. You are in the right place if you are passionate about tech, creativity, and making a real impact.
The Role: As our Social Media and Digital Engagement Coordinator, your day-to-day work involves being at the heart of our digital community. You will create engaging content, interact with our users, and analyze the buzz around our tech to help us innovate and improve. Here is what you will do:

Content Creation: Craft compelling content for our social media platforms, including Instagram, Twitter, TikTok, and LinkedIn. Think eye-catching graphics, thought-provoking posts, and videos that tell our story and showcase our tech.

Community Engagement: Be the voice of InnovateTech online. Respond to comments and messages and engage in conversations. Your goal? To build relationships and create a vibrant, supportive online community.

Trend Analysis: Stay current with digital trends, tech news, and social media evolutions. Use this insight to advise on content strategy and ensure we are always ahead of the curve.

Feedback Loop: Act as the bridge between our community and product teams. Gather insights, questions, and feedback from social media and funnel them back to help shape our products and services.

Campaign Management: From ideation to execution, manage social media campaigns that align with our goals. Track their success, analyze the data, and learn what works best.

You are Perfect for This Role If:

- You are a digital native who lives and breathes social media.
- Creativity runs in your veins – you love designing posts, shooting videos, and writing resonating content.
- Analyzing data to uncover insights and trends excites you.
- You are passionate about technology and its potential to change the world.

We Offer:

1. A fully remote and flexible working environment – work where and when you are at your best.
2. A competitive salary and benefits package, including health, dental, and vision insurance.
3. Mental health days and a strong emphasis on work-life balance.
4. Opportunities for professional development and career growth.
5. A chance to be part of a company that's shaping the future of technology.

How to Apply:

Send us your resume, tell us your story and why you are excited about this role, and provide links of any social media profiles or content you have created that you are proud of. Email everything to careers@innovatetech.com with "Social Media and Digital Engagement Coordinator" in the subject line or drop us a message on WhatsApp.

Join Us:

At InnovateTech, you are not just taking a job but joining a mission. If you want to be part of something big, something that matters, and something that's changing the world, we want you.

DIFFERENCES BETWEEN GEN Z AND BOOMER TARGETING: JOB DESCRIPTIONS

1. **Work Environment and Flexibility**:

   ◦ Gen Z: Emphasizes flexibility, remote working options, and a dynamic work environment.
   ◦ Boomers: Highlight stable, on-site work environments with traditional working hours.

2. **Company Values and Culture**:

   ◦ Gen Z: Focuses on diversity, social impact, and innovative culture.
   ◦ Boomers: Emphasize tradition, company history, and a strong sense of community.

3. **Professional Development**:

   ◦ Gen Z: Highlights opportunities for growth, learning, personal development, and precise tasks within the role.
   ◦ Boomers: Might focus more on job security, benefits, and clear role definitions.

4. **Technological Integration**:

   ◦ Gen Z: Stresses the use of technology and digital tools and stays ahead of trends.
   ◦ Boomers: Tend to value role-specific skills and experience.

5. **Social Impact**:

   ○ Gen Z: Details the company's commitment to positively impacting society or the environment.

   ○ Boomers: Are less likely to focus on social impact and instead highlight the company's market position and reliability.

6. **Language and Tone**:

   ○ Gen Z: Uses modern, relatable language that resonates with younger individuals.

   ○ Boomers: Use more formal language, highlighting respect, loyalty, and professionalism.

7. **Application Process**:

   ○ Gen Z: Has transparent, streamlined, and inclusive application processes, ideally through a platform that identifies the application stage.

   ○ Boomers: Have traditional application processes with an emphasis on experience and tenure.

Flip the Script: 3 Ideas to Consider for Crafting Job Descriptions

Scarcity Language: There is an intriguing generational dichotomy in job market perceptions, namely, older generations associate the scarcity of job openings and the detailed nature of professional job descriptions with higher salaries and greater employee loyalty and commitment (Walker & Hinojosa, 2014). However, this language and approach may alienate younger generations, who might view such descriptors as indicative of an inflexible and outdated corporate culture.

Self-assessment Language: Job postings that adopt a screening-oriented focus, delineate required qualifications comprehensively, and enable potential applicants to self-assess their fit (Dineen & Williamson, 2012). This method has been proven to significantly enhance the applicant pool's quality. However, this strategy presents a paradox for engaging Gen Z candidates, who, at their career's nascent stage, prioritize opportunities for learning and growth over immediate qualification matches.

Aesthetics: The impact of website aesthetics on organizational perception introduces a nuanced challenge for managers and executives. While an aesthetically appealing recruitment interface can attract applicants, overemphasizing visual design over substantive content may skew candidate perceptions away from the critical attributes of job roles and the organizational ethos (Lyons & Marler, 2011). Interestingly, the appeal of aesthetics is more pronounced among the younger generations, suggesting that visual strategies in recruitment might have generational preferences.

HOW TO CREATE JOB DESCRIPTIONS FOR GEN Z CANDIDATES

1. **Flexibility and Work-Life Balance**:
   - Emphasize the ability to work remotely or offer flexible working hours.
   - Mention any policies that support work-life balance, such as mental health days, wellness meetings, or no-email weekends.

2. **Promote Company Culture and Values**:
   - Clearly state the company's commitment to diversity, inclusion, and social responsibility.
   - Describe the company culture as collaborative, innovative, and dynamic.

3. **Focus on Professional Development**:
   - Include opportunities for growth, such as mentorship programs, workshops, access to online courses, and on-demand information.
   - Highlight how the role allows for creative freedom and personal development.
   - If possible, ensure they have a mentor to teach them the ropes – explicitly state this opportunity.

4. **Emphasize Digital and Modern Work Environment**:
   - Mention using the latest technologies and digital tools in daily operations.

    ◦ Highlight any innovative projects or cutting-edge fields the company is involved in.

5. **Detail the Social Impact**:

    ◦ Explain how the company's work contributes to positive social or environmental change.

    ◦ Provide examples of past initiatives or projects that made a difference.

6. **Include Collaboration and Community**:

    ◦ Describe how the role involves teamwork and collaboration.

    ◦ Mention any team-building activities, community events, or clubs within the company.

7. **Be Transparent About the Application Process**:

    ◦ Provide a clear and straightforward application process.

    ◦ Encourage applications from all backgrounds to promote diversity.

8. **Use Modern, Relatable Language**:

    ◦ Avoid corporate jargon and opt for a more conversational tone.

    ◦ Use language that resonates with younger generations.

    ◦ Write in bullets whenever possible.

9. **Detail Expectations and Design**

    ◦ Articulate expectations and how these will be measured.

    ◦ Detail specific tasks and methods for prioritizing tasks.

    ◦ If possible, specify the hourly rate from the start.

CONCLUSIONS

Recognizing the pivotal role of job descriptions as strategic assets, not merely informational tools, businesses can significantly influence the caliber and fit of applicants. A strategic, thoughtful creation of job ads aligned with Generation Z's values, expectations, and language can transform recruitment from a passive process into a dynamic engagement strategy. This approach positions organizations as desirable employers and attracts talent that aligns with their goals and culture, thereby enhancing recruitment outcomes for both parties.

Undergoing a Gen Z Job Description Audit followed by the implementation of Gen Z targeted language ensures job descriptions resonate with this demographic. Organizations can create compelling job descriptions by highlighting innovation, diversity, flexibility, and social responsibility, aligning job titles, summaries, and responsibilities with Gen Z's language and values. Furthermore, emphasizing work-life balance, professional development opportunities, and a modern, digital work environment can appeal to Gen Z candidates, fostering a dynamic and future-ready workforce. Through such strategic adjustments, leaders can navigate the complexities of attracting Gen Z talent, ensuring their organizations remain competitive and innovative in the rapidly changing business landscape.

Box 9.2 Critical Take-Aways for Chapter 9

1   **Flex Your Flexibility:** Showcase the work environment's elasticity and embrace innovation in the job description;

2   **Growth Is on the Agenda:** Explain that the role is not just a position but a journey. Highlight mentorship, learning resources, and clear career pathways to signal to Gen Z that professional evolution is essential;

3   **Diversity Is not Just a Buzzword:** Go beyond mere declarations of diversity and inclusion; illuminate your active commitments and vibrant company culture that celebrates all voices.

NOTES

1   See Walker and Hinojosa (2014) for an in-depth literature analysis on recruitment.

2   The name of the company is fictional to maintain confidentiality.

REFERENCES

Allen, D. G., Scotter, J. R. V., & Otondo, R. F. (2004). Recruitment communication media: Impact on prehire outcomes. *Personnel Psychology*, *57*(1), 143–171. https://doi.org/10.1111/j.1744-6570.2004.tb02487.x.

Avery, D. R. (2003). Reactions to diversity in recruitment advertising—Are differences black and white? *Journal of Applied Psychology*, *88*(4), 672–679. https://doi.org/10.1037/0021-9010.88.4.672.

Brown, D. J., Cober, R. T., Keeping, L. M., & Levy, P. E. (2006). Racial tolerance and reactions to diversity information in job advertisements1 *Journal of Applied Social Psychology*, *36*(8), 2048–2071. https://doi.org/10.1111/j.0021-9029.2006.00093.x.

Dineen, B. R., & Soltis, S. M. (2011). Recruitment: A review of research and emerging directions. In S. Zedeck (Ed.), *APA handbook of industrial and organizational psychology, Vol 2: Selecting and developing members for the organization* (pp. 43–66). American Psychological Association. https://doi.org/10.1037/12170-002.

Dineen, B. R., & Williamson, I. O. (2012). Screening-oriented recruitment messages: Antecedents and relationships with applicant pool quality. *Human Resource Management*, *51*(3), 343–360. https://doi.org/10.1002/hrm.21476.

Gatewood, R. D., Gowan, M. A., & Lautenschlager, G. J. (1993). Corporate image, recruitment image, and initial job choice decisions. *Academy of Management Journal*, *36*(2), 414–427. https://doi.org/10.5465/256530.

Highhouse, S., Brooks, M. E., & Gregarus, G. (2009). An organizational impression management perspective on the formation of corporate reputations. *Journal of Management*, *35*(6), 1481–1493. https://doi.org/10.1177/0149206309348788.

James, E. H., Brief, A. P., Dietz, J., & Cohen, R. R. (2001). Prejudice matters: Understanding the reactions of Whites to affirmative action programs targeted to benefit Blacks. *Journal of Applied Psychology*, *86*(6), 1120–1128. https://doi.org/10.1037/0021-9010.86.6.1120.

Lyons, B. D., & Marler, J. H. (2011). Got image? Examining organizational image in web recruitment. *Journal of Managerial Psychology*, *26*(1), 58–76. https://doi.org/10.1108/02683941111099628.

Reeve, C. L., & Schultz, L. (2004). Job-seeker reactions to selection process information in job Ads. *International Journal of Selection and Assessment*, *12*(4), 343–355. https://doi.org/10.1111/j.0965-075X.2004.00289.x.

Thorsteinson, T. J., & Highhouse, S. (2003). Effects of goal framing in job advertisements on organizational attractiveness1 *Journal of Applied Social Psychology*, *33*(11), 2393–2412. https://doi.org/10.1111/j.1559-1816.2003. tb01891.x.

Walker, H. J., Feild, H. S., Giles, W. F., Armenakis, A. A., & Bernerth, J. B. (2009). Displaying employee testimonials on recruitment web sites: Effects of communication media, employee race, and job seeker race on organizational attraction and information credibility. *Journal of Applied Psychology*, *94*(5), 1354–1364. https://doi.org/10.1037/a0014964

Walker, H. J., Feild, H. S., Giles, W. F., Bernerth, J. B., & Jones-Farmer, L. A. (2007). An assessment of attraction toward affirmative action organizations: Investigating the role of individual differences. *Journal of Organizational Behavior*, *28*(4), 485–507. https://doi.org/10.1002/job.434.

Walker, H. J., & Hinojosa, A. S. (2014). Recruitment: The role of job advertisements. In *The Oxford handbook of recruitment* (pp. 269–283). Oxford University Press.

HOW TO ONBOARD GEN Z
EMPLOYEES

Abstract

This chapter introduces the Gen Z Employee Onboarding and Integration Framework and outlines a comprehensive onboarding process for Gen Z employees. From the initial phase of pre-onboarding, where evident, realistic job descriptions set the stage for success, to the crucial moments of evaluation and assimilation, each stage provides actionable advice crafted to ensure a seamless transition and foster long-term engagement.

Key take-aways underscore the necessity of a structured yet flexible onboarding process, the value of mentorship and peer support systems, and the critical role of continuous feedback and professional development. This strategic blueprint preempts the discourse on 'quiet quitting' phenomenon and leverages Gen Z's dynamic energy and innovative potential, positioning organizations for future growth and success. By implementing this framework, leaders and managers are equipped to cultivate a workforce that is engaged, productive, and aligned with the organization's objectives.

Box 10.1 Onboarding and Integration Audit

To the Reader:

The Gen Z Onboarding and Integration Audit is a comprehensive tool designed for modern managers committed to creating an engaging, supportive, and productive workplace for the newest generation

---

DOI: 10.4324/9781032722696-12

entering the workforce. This audit is based on the latest research and best practices tailored to meet Generation Z employees' unique needs and expectations. The audit is intended to help practicing managers evaluate whether they are effectively onboarding Gen Z employees.

Gen Z Onboarding and Integration Audit

1 Pre-Onboarding:

- ☐ Have realistic job descriptions been provided to reduce early disillusionment?
- ☐ Is there clear communication between the time of hire and the start date?
- ☐ Are intrinsic rewards and a sense of job fit communicated to engage Gen Z before they start?

2 Onboarding:

- ☐ Is there an effective orientation process that covers rights, obligations, work expectations, workflow, and department overviews?
- ☐ Are new hires assigned a mentor and a "buddy" to help them adapt to and transition into the company?
- ☐ Do the onboarding materials and activities engage Gen Z preferences for interactive and digital content?

3 Probation Period:

- ☐ Can new employees undertake level-appropriate tasks and actively participate in meetings and activities?
- ☐ Is there a system allowing new hires the autonomy to decide if they want to continue with the company?
- ☐ After probation, are there opportunities for in-depth training, more responsibilities, and comparable rewards to experienced employees?

4 Evaluation:

- ☐ Are there regular reviews of the new hire's progress, job descriptions, and workload adjustments? Is there a combination of formal and informal evaluation methods, such as

annual reviews, daily check-ins, and participative meetings?
☐ Are evaluations designed to enhance competence and manage stress levels effectively?

5 Assimilation:

☐ Once fully integrated, are employees provided with opportunities for job enrichment and increased autonomy?
☐ Can assimilated employees mentor new hires, contributing to
a cycle of continuous improvement and engagement?
☐ Are there measures to maintain mentorship and ensure
ongoing support and guidance?

6 Continuous Follow-Up:

☐ Is there a structured approach for new hires to clarify misun-
derstandings and provide feedback?
☐ Are there regular check-ins to ensure new hires integrate well
and address any issues promptly?
☐ Do follow-up actions align with the engagement dimensions
of job redesign, enrichment, and social rewards?

In the contemporary corporate arena, many firms grapple with
fragmented employee integration systems, a challenge that undermines
the holistic onboarding experience. The strategic framework proposed
herein synthesizes insights on employee integration, enriched with
findings pertinent to the intricacies of Generation Z engagement. This
fusion aims to architect a more structured, cohesive integration journey, as underscored by the principles of Multigenerational Leadership,
which prioritizes the nuanced engagement of diverse generational
cohorts.

By harmonizing specific integration actions with the distinct
engagement dimensions of Generation Z, leaders can usher in a new
era of workplace harmony and productivity. The benefits of such a
refined integration process are manifold. First, it fosters a stronger
sense of belonging and alignment with the company's mission among
new hires, as illustrated by the improved retention rates (Jones, 1986;

Weinstock, 2015). Second, a tailored integration approach catalyzes quicker assimilation into productivity streams, enhancing overall operational efficiency (Lynch & Buckner-Hayden, 2010). This strategic alignment between employee expectations and organizational objectives leads to heightened team innovation and creativity, tapping into unique strengths and perspectives (Baker & DiPiro, 2019).

For leaders and managers, the mandate is clear: to embrace and implement a cohesive integration strategy that resonates with Generation Z's expectations and amplifies their potential within the organizational fabric. Committing to such a process is not merely a strategic advantage but a necessity in the age of rapid generational turnover.

FROM THEORY TO PRACTICE: TRANSLATING ONBOARDING THEORIES INTO ACTION

In the ever-evolving landscape of employee integration, two distinct approaches have historically dominated the conversation: institutionalized versus individualized socialization (Jones, 1986). Institutionalized methods, characterized by a structured step-by-step induction including orientation and mentorship, contrast sharply with individualized strategies, where new employees navigate their learning journey independently. The effectiveness of standardized frameworks has significantly influenced employee success rates within organizations (Baker & DiPiro, 2019; Lynch & Buckner-Hayden, 2010; Weinstock, 2015).

Comprehensive organizational integration programs extend beyond job functionality to encapsulate the business's overarching culture and core values (Pike, 2014). This multifaceted approach to integration – spanning pre-onboarding to follow-up – plays a critical role in fostering an understanding of the company's culture, network building, and strategic career development (Stein & Christiansen, 2010).

A nuanced enhancement to traditional onboarding practices responds to the emerging needs of younger generations entering the workforce. Pairing new hires with seasoned organizational mentors and "buddies" – peers of a similar age or career stage – facilitates a more relatable and supportive transition into the corporate environment (Klinghoffer & Kirkpatrick-Husk, 2023).

The digital savviness of these younger cohorts has also catalyzed a transformative shift towards gamified integration strategies (Depura & Garg, 2012; Heimburger et al., 2019). Research on the influence of gamified integration on employee engagement indicates that Generations Y and Z prefer gamified onboarding to non-gamified onboarding (Heimburger et al., 2019). Technologically integrated workspaces with up-to-date software, mobile applications, and gamification appear to improve the success of young employee integration (Depura & Garg, 2012). Businesses can create engaging and technologically resonant onboarding experiences by incorporating game elements into non-gaming contexts (Dale, 2014). This innovative approach caters to the preferences of Generations Y and Z and bridges the gap between engagement and leadership within information systems.

For business leaders and practicing managers, the imperative is to harness these insights and methodologies to forge a more adaptive, inclusive, and practical integration process. Table 10.1 aims to serve as a guide, offering actionable strategies and insights that align with the modern workforce's unique needs and expectations. It also describes Gen Z's engagement dimension attained through the proposed methods.

PRE-ONBOARDING: SETTING THE STAGE FOR SUCCESS

The journey begins even before the new hire sets foot in the office. Pre-onboarding is the foundational phase where Gen Z candidates evaluate the role and the organization (Dharmasiri et al., 2014). Here, clarity reigns supreme. Realistic job descriptions are not just descriptions; they are the first line of communication that can foster alignment or seed disillusionment. Unrealistic descriptions can lead to disillusionment (Dharmasiri et al., 2014). This stage is pivotal for setting accurate expectations and facilitating a smooth transition into the company culture. During this phase, Generation Z employees assess intrinsic rewards and perceived job fit based on realistic job descriptions.

Table 10.1 Generation Z Integration Process

Stages	Actions	Employee Collaboration Dynamic	Engagement Dimensions Attained
Stage 1: Pre-on-boarding.	Offer realistic job descriptions and top management greetings.	Experienced employee as a mentor.	Intrinsic rewards; Social rewards.
Stage 2: Onboarding.	2.1 Orientation.	Receive employee handbook and information materials; tour departments; explain expectations; job description; present expectations.	An employee of the same age or Gen Y as a buddy.	Empowerment; Social rewards.
Stage 3: Proba-tion period.	2.2 Organizational socialization.	Culture, network development, career development, strategy communication.		
	3.1 Employee undertakes level-appropriate skills.		Experienced employee as a mentor.	Empowerment; Choice; Personal engagement.
	3.2 Employees partake in meetings and expand job design.		An employee of the same age or Gen Y as a buddy.	
Stage 4: Integra-tion.	In-depth training; Employee receives more responsibilities; Similar financial and workload to more experienced employees.	Experienced employee as a mentor.	Empowerment; Enrichment External rewards.
		An employee of the same age or Gen Y as a buddy.	

Continued

Table 10.1 (Continued)

Stages	Actions	Employee Collaboration Dynamic	Engagement Dimensions Attained
Stage 5: Evaluation.	Reports of managers, Self-evaluations; questionnaires, surveys; KPIs; results, evaluation meetings.	Experienced employee as a mentor. An employee of the same age or Gen Y as a buddy.	Competence; Stress-level maintenance.
Stage 6: Assimilation.	Career development; Variation of work; Becoming a buddy for new hire.	Experienced employee as a mentor.	Enrichment, Job design, Social rewards.
Stage 7: Follow-up.	Continuous follow-up, Sensemaking, expectations management, Periodic check-ins.	Experienced employee as a mentor.	Empowerment.

ONBOARDING: CRAFTING AN APPROPRIATE IMPRESSION

The formal onboarding phase, encompassing orientation and organizational socialization, is where the real introduction to the company begins. It encompasses more than just orientation; it is about integrating the new hire into the organization's fabric. This phase should be structured yet flexible, combining traditional elements like handbooks and workflows with personalized mentorship and buddy systems (Klinghoffer et al., 2019). These initial interactions are crucial for instilling a sense of empowerment and belonging as the building blocks for long-term engagement. With a personalized mentor, the new hire can receive guidance and support throughout and after onboarding (Klinghoffer et al., 2019). This helps instill a sense of empowerment and belonging, crucial building blocks for long-term engagement. Furthermore, the buddy system pairs the new hire with an experienced employee from either Generation Z or Y (Klinghoffer et al., 2019). This allows the new employee to adapt to the company's culture and work environment. By having someone to help them navigate the social dynamics of the organization, the new hire experiences empowerment and social rewards.

PROBATION PERIOD: EMPOWERMENT AND EXPLORATION

The pre-determined probation period represents a critical testing ground for the employee and the organization. It is a time for practical engagement, where the new hire can immerse themselves in tasks, contribute to meetings, and gauge the fit with the company. This period should encourage exploration and offer a safety net, enabling the young employees to make an informed decision about their place within the organization. The aim is to transition from mere adaptation to genuine contribution, fostering a sense of enrichment and value. After probation, the new employee undergoes in-depth training, takes on more responsibilities, and receives rewards similar to those experienced employees for comparable work. This stage allows the new employee to grow and receive external rewards.

EVALUATION: CONTINUOUS GROWTH

Evaluation is an ongoing dialogue, not a checkpoint. Practical evaluation encompassing technical and soft skills should merge structured assessments with informal check-ins. This blend ensures comprehensive and approachable feedback, facilitating personal and professional growth. Moreover, this stage is about calibration – adjusting job descriptions, expectations, and support to align with the individual's progress and aspirations. Various tools like reports, results, surveys, questionnaires, and performance reviews are employed, with formal and informal methods, such as daily check-ins and participative meetings. Evaluation not only enhances competence but also contributes to Gen Z's stress management.

ASSIMILATION: CULTIVATING LONG-TERM ENGAGEMENT

Post-evaluation, the journey of assimilation begins. Here, the focus shifts to deeper integration within the team and the broader organizational context. Job enrichment and increased autonomy play significant roles as the now-assimilated Gen Z employee begins to navigate the landscape more confidently and independently. It is also a stage where reciprocity comes into play – the new hire, having been mentored, may now become a buddy for subsequent newcomers, perpetuating a culture of continuous learning.

FOLLOW-UP: CONTINUOUS CHECK-INS AND FEEDBACK LOOPS

Regular check-ins are pivotal in the follow-up phase, providing Gen Z employees with a platform to voice concerns, ask questions, and receive feedback. This practice should transcend routine status updates, fostering an open dialogue where feedback is bidirectional. Managers should utilize these check-ins to gauge the employee's comfort level, understand their challenges, and recognize their achievements. Establishing a regular schedule for these discussions, whether weekly or biweekly, can help Gen Z employees feel valued and listened to, thereby enhancing their engagement and commitment to the organization.

Box 10.2 Ensuring Rapid Integration: A Manager's Role

For contemporary business leaders, implementing a nuanced onboarding framework transcends mere procedure – it signifies a fundamental shift towards active engagement with the workforce's newest members. This shift is not about adhering to a prescriptive set of tasks but about fostering an organizational culture where dialogue, development, and innovation are at the forefront. By championing these values, managers catalyze the transformation of Gen Z talent into formidable organizational pillars.

In the current business landscape, many organizations face the challenge of fragmented employee integration practices, often leading to inconsistent and ineffective onboarding experiences. This fragmented approach undermines the employee's integration experience and diminishes organizational cohesion and efficiency. The integrated approach proposed here is rooted in a blend of established research and new insights into Gen Z's unique engagement needs. By aligning the onboarding process with these insights, companies can forge a more coherent and impactful integration journey.

The stakes are high as traditional methods have failed to address the phenomenon of 'quiet quitting' – a passive withdrawal from active engagement without leaving the job. This lackluster engagement can severely truncate the tenure and productivity of Gen Z employees. By reimagining the integration process, organizations can preemptively address the precursors of disengagement, extending the productive and active phase of Gen Z's employment lifecycle.

Adopting a more resource-efficient and targeted onboarding strategy does more than prolong tenure; it harnesses the dynamism and zeal characteristic of the Gen Z cohort during their most energetic "activist and diehard" phases. This approach not only bolsters the individual's commitment and contribution but also amplifies the collective energy and innovation within the team.

In essence, this enhanced integration framework offers two benefits: it secures a more engaged and productive workforce and propels the organization toward a future marked by innovation, agility, and sustained growth.

CONCLUSIONS

This chapter underscores the imperative of adopting modern onboarding strategies that resonate with Generation Z's unique dynamics. The transition from pre-onboarding to complete assimilation emerges not as a mere procedure but as a complex journey requiring adaptability, commitment, and active engagement from managers and leaders.

The Gen Z Onboarding and Integration Framework provides a comprehensive blueprint for this critical journey. It is a strategic guide designed to assist managers in creating an environment where Gen Z employees can excel, bringing innovation and significant contributions to the forefront.

The necessity for a unified approach to integration is underscored; an ad-hoc strategy leads to disengagement and high turnover, while a coherent, Gen Z-focused strategy fosters a vibrant, innovative, and committed employee base. Aligning organizational practices with Gen Z's motivations prevents the pitfalls of 'quiet quitting' and promotes a more prosperous, more engaging workplace culture.

This chapter, thus, acts not merely as a compendium of best practices but as an imperative for action. For leaders steering through the intricacies of multigenerational leadership, the Gen Z Onboarding and Integration Audit is introduced as an essential mechanism for evaluation and enhancement.

Box 10.3 Key Take-Aways for Chapter 10

1 **Provide Mentorship and Peer Support**: Pairing Gen Z employees with experienced mentors and peers (buddies) from their generation or Generation Y facilitates smoother integration, provides valuable guidance, and fosters a sense of belonging and community within the organization;

2 **Generate Continuous Feedback and Development**: Implementing a robust feedback mechanism and providing ongoing development opportunities are essential for maintaining Gen Z's motivation and commitment. Regular evaluations and follow-ups help address their needs for growth, recognition, and constructive feedback, leading to improved job satisfaction and retention;

3 **Produce Immediate Access to Learning**: Providing on-demand information allows employees to resolve queries and challenges in real-time, significantly enhancing their productivity and fostering a culture of continuous learning and improvement.

REFERENCES

Baker, B., & DiPiro, J. T. (2019). Evaluation of a structured onboarding process and tool for faculty members in a school of pharmacy. *American Journal of Pharmaceutical Education, 83*(6), 7100.

Dale, S. (2014). Gamification: Making work fun, or making fun of work? *Business Information Review, 31*(2), 82–90. https://doi.org/10.1177/0266382114538350.

Depura, K., & Garg, M. (2012). Application of online gamification to new hire onboarding. *Third International Conference on Services in Emerging Markets*, 153–156. https://doi.org/10.1109/ICSEM.2012.29.

Dharmasiri, A., Buckley, M., Baur, J., & Sahatjian, Z. (2014). A historical approach to realistic job previews. *Journal of Management History, 20*, https://doi.org/10.1108-06-2012-0046.

Heimburger, L., Buchweitz, L., Gouveia, R., & Korn, O. (2019). Gamifying onboarding: How to increase both engagement and integration of new employees. In R. Goossens & A. Murata (Eds.), *Advances in social and occupational ergonomics. AHFE 2019. Advances in intelligent systems and computing* (Vol. 970). Springer. https://doi.org/10.1007/978-3-030-20145-6_1.

Jones, G. R. (1986). Socialization tactics, self-efficacy, and newcomers' adjustments to organizations. *Academy of Management Journal, 29*(2), 262–279. https://www.jstor.org/stable/256188

Klinghoffer, D., & Kirkpatrick-Husk, K. (2023, May 18). More than 50% of managers feel burned out. *Harvard Business Review.* https://hbr.org/2023/05/more-than-50-of-managers-feel-burned-out

Klinghoffer, D., Young, C., & Haspas, D. (2019). Every new employee needs an onboarding buddy. *Harvard Business Review.* https://hbr.org/2019/06/every-new-employee-needs-an-onboarding-buddy

Lynch, K., & Buckner-Hayden, G. (2010). Reducing the new employee learning curve to improve productivity. *Journal of Healthcare Risk Management. The Journal of the American Society for Healthcare Risk Management, 29*(3), 22–28. https://doi.org/10.1002/jhrm.20020.

Pike, K. L. (2014). New employee onboarding programs and person-organization fit: An examination of socialization tactics. In *Seminar Research Paper Series. Paper 24.* https://digitalcommons.uri.edu/cgi/viewcontent.cgi?-referer=https://www.google.com/&httpsredir=1&article=1043&context=lrc_paper_series

Stein, M., & Christiansen, L. (2010). *Successful onboarding: Strategies to unlock hidden value within your organization.* McGraw Hill.

Weinstock, D. (2015). Hiring new staff? Aim for success by onboarding. *The Journal of Medical Practice Management, 31*(2), 96–98. https://www.proquest.com/openview/4b7934d172750aefa3e4036af9a8dd92/1?pq-origsite=gscholar&cbl=32264

WHY ARE GEN Z DISENGAGED?

Abstract

This chapter explores the reasons behind Gen Z's disengagement and introduces the Three Forces of Disengagement and the 3D Disengagement Model. This analysis delves into the pervasive issue of Generation Z disengagement in the workplace, unveiling the nuanced interplay of factors that detract from their engagement and productivity. At the core of this examination lies the Three Forces of Disengagement Model, which serves as a lens to understand the unique challenges Generation Z employees face.

Disengagement surfaces under unfair workload distribution, lack of recognition, and restrictive decision-making autonomy. The narrative extends into power dynamics within the multigenerational workforce, spotlighting the stark contrasts in power access between older generations and Generation Z. This disparity often leaves younger employees feeling marginalized, prompting them to exit the workplace in a trend increasingly identified as "ghosting."

In the complex landscape of the contemporary workplace, the challenge of understanding and counteracting Gen Z disengagement has become a pivotal focus for business leaders and managers. To navigate this terrain effectively, it is essential to dissect the elements that fuel engagement and those that foster disengagement among this youngest cohort of employees.

Responses collated from managerial experiences, alongside first-hand accounts from Gen Z workers, depicted in Table 11.1,[1] offer insights into the engagement conditions and drivers. These insights

DOI: 10.4324/9781032722696-13

Table 11.1 Responses Collated from Managers and Gen Z Workers.

Category	*Responses Summary*
Conditions for Engagement	Engagement occurs when one is empowered by coworkers and managers when one can feel their trust and support and when there is collegiality, transparency, and a positive atmosphere. Also, receiving praise, financial rewards, and status is empowering. The employee not only has to be competent in the domain but also has to like the work and to experience progress. One must promptly receive precise tasks and instructions from an engaged manager and training and development. One has to be rested, and the stress levels caused by multitasking are minimal.
Conditions for Disengagement	Disengagement occurs when the workload or the schedule is unfairly distributed, the manager takes advantage of employees, or there is increased stress and pressure. Disengagement is also related to a hostile atmosphere, misunderstandings, marginalization, and favoritism. It stems from a lack of choice and little decision-making power. It is related to one's work being underappreciated, low wages, lack of progress or impact, and general indifference. It may also happen when errors are committed, and the employee feels incompetent, or when they dread going to work or "feel" they are being in the wrong workplace.

reveal that Gen Z engagement thrives in environments characterized by empowerment, trust, and support from both colleagues and managers. A culture of collegiality, transparency, and positivity significantly boosts their motivation, as does recognition through praise, financial incentives, and advancement opportunities. For Gen Z, feeling competent and valued and seeing tangible progress in their work are crucial factors. Clear, timely instructions, coupled with opportunities for training and personal development, further enhance their engagement. Additionally, maintaining a balanced workload and minimizing stress from multitasking are fundamental to keeping Gen Z employees focused and content.

Conversely, disengagement among Gen Z employees can stem from various workplace conditions. Unfair task distribution, managerial exploitation, heightened stress, and toxic workplace culture are the primary culprits. Feelings of marginalization, favoritism, or lack of autonomy can exacerbate this disengagement, as can feelings of underappreciation or stagnation in their roles. Financial dissatisfaction, perceived tactlessness, and the fear of incompetence can also lead to a disengaged Gen Z workforce. When Gen Z employees dread coming to work or feel they are in the wrong environment, disengagement is inevitable.

The dichotomy between engagement and disengagement in Gen Z highlights a crucial managerial strategy: enhancing favorable workplace conditions while mitigating negative ones. The neutral dimensions – such as job enrichment, job design, and management style – serve as additional levers for engagement. While enhancing these aspects can propel Gen Z employees towards greater engagement, their absence does not inherently result in disengagement. This nuanced understanding compels managers to adopt a balanced approach, emphasizing both the promotion of engagement drivers and the reduction of disengagement factors – illustrated in Figure 11.1.

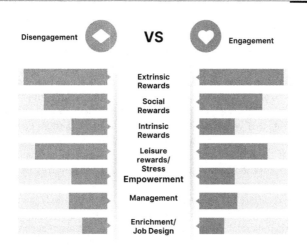

COMPARISON CHART ENGAGEMENT DIMENSIONS

Disengagement VS Engagement

Extrinsic Rewards

Social Rewards

Intrinsic Rewards

Leisure rewards/ Stress

Empowerment

Management

Enrichment/ Job Design

Figure 11.1 Gen Z Engagement and Disengagement Conditions.
Source: Figure by author.

In essence, the path to Gen Z engagement is multifaceted. Managers must craft strategies that elevate the positive dimensions of the workplace and systematically address and eliminate the root causes of disengagement. The remainder of this chapter will primarily consider disengagement factors.

THE 3D DISENGAGEMENT MODEL

Box 11.1 The Forces of Disengagement

Three organizational forces lead to Gen Z disengagement:

1   *Unrealistic expectations:* Many lower-level Gen Z-ers come to work expecting rapid rewards that only time and diligence will typically earn.

    Young employees reach the workplace with unrealistic expectations – often because of the influencer culture that models a life of fast achievement. Young recruits desire fast rewards in the form of pay and generous praise. Tenured employees expect young ones to demonstrate consistent effort over time – an idea that baffles recruits and makes them think they are oppressed in the workplace.

2   *Generational conflict:* Mid-level Boomers often need to be more inclined to show Gen Z the ropes; fearing their jobs, they willingly or unwillingly keep young recruits helpless.

    Tenured employees in many organizations need to be more inclined to teach young employees the ropes out of fear for their jobs. While verbally tenured employees will appear to support the education of young employees, in practice, they often oppose initiatives that would position young employees in a more powerful position. For instance, the predominant strength of young employees is their technological capability. Yet, most tenured employees oppose technologization out of fear of losing their increased organizational control.

3   *Power differentials in the workplace* – the most critical source of Gen Z angst: Boomers and Gen X generally have all the power due to their hierarchical positions, experience, and years of service. The only power available to Gen Z employees is the rewards, recognition, and praise they crave but seldom get as quickly as expected.

Gen Z-ers resent their lack of power, and their companies usually do not have systems in place to address the issue.

Companies are slow to rebalance power; they would rather complain about young employees not accepting "how things are done around here." Intergenerational management and human resources systems that consider the special needs of young employees are almost nonexistent within companies. At the organizational governance level, boards do not offer the necessary intergenerational support, leaving managers to fend for themselves.

Power Distribution Among the Workforce

The landscape of the modern workplace is undergoing a seismic shift in power dynamics, challenging the traditional paradigms that have long governed organizational hierarchies. At the pinnacle of this transformation is the need to reconcile the divergent power bases across different generations, particularly as Generation Z begins to carve out its space in the corporate world.

All employees exhibit some will to power and wish to address it in the workplace.[2] Generational groups are perceived to be able to access different bases of power.[3] Historically, power has predominantly resided with the seasoned professionals – now Boomers and Generation X – due to their depth of experience, hierarchical status, and, in many cases, equity stakes. This group wields substantial influence, shaping organizational policies and dictating the strategic direction (Kupperschmidt, 2000). Meanwhile, Millennials and, more recently, Generation Z navigate a landscape where their aspirations for rapid advancement and recognition clash with the existing power structures.

The advent of the Power and Multigenerational Workforce Model marks a significant leap toward understanding these complex dynamics. This model (see Figure 11.2) underscores that while older generations possess comprehensive forms of power, including legitimate, expert, and coercive, the younger cohorts often find themselves relegated to seeking "prestige power" – a form of reward characterized by acknowledgment and validation, yet elusive and rarely offered to younger recruits by tenured employees.

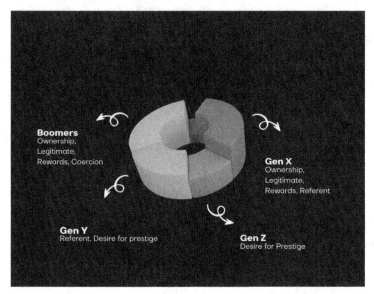

Figure 11.2 Power Distribution Among the Workforce.
Source: Figure by author.

The repercussions of this imbalance are profound. Younger employees, feeling disenfranchised and undervalued, may opt for the drastic measure of exiting the organization – a phenomenon increasingly observed as "ghosting." This trend highlights a critical gap in the traditional power schema, where the lack of empowerment and recognition leaves the younger workforce disenchanted and disengaged. Generation Z employees find themselves at a distinct disadvantage when wielding the sophisticated influence tactics that their senior counterparts command, a result of years in the workforce and the nuanced understanding of organizational dynamics this brings. Faced with this disparity, their recourse often boils down to an intensified effort to prove their worth over time, a concept met with resistance by young recruits (Lancaster & Stillman, 2003; Tolbize, 2008; Twenge et al., 2010; Urick et al., 2017). This reluctance paves the way for their ultimate form of protest: withdrawal from the workplace. This departure, often abrupt and without forewarning – "ghosting" – stands as a testament to the unique challenges and perceptions of power by Generation Z in today's work environment.

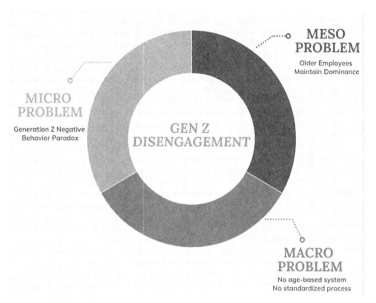

Figure 11.3 3D Model of Disengagement.

Source: Figure by author.

However, the solution lies beyond merely addressing the symptoms of this generational power divide. It demands a revaluation of how power is distributed and exercised within organizations. Leaders are called upon to cultivate an environment where power extends beyond tenure and titles to one where it is equally accessible, promoting a culture of mutual respect, learning, and recognition (Figure 11.3).

The 3D Power Disengagement Model

The 3D Power Disengagement Model for Generation Z stems from the combination of three dimensions as follows:

1. At an individual level, Generation Z employees experience The Negative Behavior Paradox and are in a Job Crisis Loop, as discussed in Chapter 7.
2. At an organizational level, older employees maintain dominance and position by willingly or unwillingly oppressing Generation Z, as previously discussed and illustrated in Figure 11.2.

3. At a systemic level, managers need to implement systems and processes to support the development of Generation Z – which they usually eschew.

The concept of 3D Disengagement has two critical implications. First, it challenges traditional power distribution methods and encourages a more collaborative and inclusive approach to leadership. Second, it helps managers better understand the current workplace and avoid confusion by describing its operational realities.

A reimagined approach to power dynamics would mitigate the risks associated with disengagement and turnover and unlock new avenues for innovation and growth. By embracing a multigenerational leadership model, organizations can harness their workforce's diverse strengths and perspectives, paving the way for a more resilient corporate culture.

CONCLUSIONS

Understanding and mitigating Gen Z disengagement in today's dynamic work environment is crucial for ensuring organizational harmony and productivity. A supportive, transparent, and empowering workplace culture, coupled with tangible recognition and professional development opportunities, has been identified as key to fostering Gen Z's engagement. Conversely, unfair work distributions, perceived managerial exploitation, and a lack of autonomy are significant disengagement catalysts, propelling Gen Z toward exit.

The Three Forces of Disengagement – unrealistic expectations, generational conflict, and power differentials – underscore today's organizations' multifaceted challenges. Influenced by a culture of rapid achievement, young employees enter the workforce with expectations misaligned with traditional career trajectories, leading to frustration and disengagement. Furthermore, the reluctance of tenured employees to empower their younger counterparts exacerbates generational tensions and stifles technological advancement and innovation. All leading to the 3D Disengagement Model.

The Power and Multigenerational Workforce Model introduces the need for a paradigm shift, urging a rebalance of power dynamics to accommodate Gen Z's aspirations and working styles. This reality calls for a departure from entrenched power hierarchies, advocating for a workplace where prestige power is accessible to all, thereby democratizing influence and decision-making.

Leaders are encouraged to recognize and address these generational disparities, fostering an environment where all employees feel valued, understood, and empowered regardless of tenure. Implementing strategies that bridge the power gap can transform organizational culture, reduce Gen Z turnover, and enhance overall workforce engagement.

Box 11.2 Key Take-Aways for Chapter 11

1 **Address and Mitigate Disengagement Factors**: Proactively identify and tackle conditions that lead to Gen Z disengagement. This includes addressing unfair workload distribution, preventing managerial exploitation, and eliminating favoritism. Create strategies to reduce stress, avoid marginalization, and ensure employees do not feel undervalued;

2 **Bridge the Generational Power Gap**: Recognize and address the power differentials between tenured employees and Gen Z workers. Create pathways for Gen Z to access "prestige power" through recognition, rewards, and opportunities for input and decision-making. Encourage knowledge-sharing and collaboration between generations to break down barriers and build mutual respect;

3 **Align Expectations with Reality**: Understand and manage Gen Z's expectations regarding their career progression and workplace rewards. Counteract the influence of a "fast achievement" culture by setting realistic goals and providing clear, constructive feedback. Foster an environment where long-term effort and resilience are valued and rewarded.

NOTES

1 The findings represented in the table are the composite summaries of the open-ended, semi-structured interviews with 30 Gen Z employees and 45 managers. Responses were codified through open and axial coding and transformed into categories using Hycner's (1999) process.

2 For the discourse on human desire for power see Nietzsche's (1968) Will to Power.

3 The bases of power considered in this work follow the classification by French and Raven (1959) with the completion of Finkelstein and Hambrick (1996).

REFERENCES

Finkelstein, S., & Hambrick, D. (1996). *Strategic leadership: Top executives and their effects on organizations*. West Pub.

French, J., & Raven, B. (1959). The bases of social power. In D. Cartwright & A. Zander (Eds.), *Group dynamics* (pp. 151–164). Harper & Row. https://www.researchgate.net/publication/215915730_The_bases_of_social_power

Hycner, R. H. (1999). Some guidelines for the phenomenological analysis of interview data. In A. Bryman, & R. G. Burgess (Eds.), *Qualitative Research* (Vol. 3, pp. 143–164). Sage.

Kupperschmidt, B. (2000). Multigeneration employees: Strategies for effective management. *The Health Care Manager*, *19*(1), 65–76. https://journals.lww.com/healthcaremanagerjournal/Citation/2000/19010/Multigeneration_Employees__Strategies_for.11.aspx

Lancaster, L. C., & Stillman, D. (2003). *When generations collide: Who they are.* Collins.

Nietzsche, F. W., Kaufmann, W., & Hollingdale, R. J. (1968). *The Will to Power*. Vintage Books ed. New York: Vintage Books.

Tolbize, A. (2008). *Generational differences in the workplace*. Research and Training Center on Community Living, University of Minnesota. https://rtc.umn.edu/docs/2_18_Gen_diff_workplace.pdf

Twenge, J., Campbell, S., Hoffman, B., & Lance, C. (2010). Generational differences in work values: Leisure and extrinsic values increasing, social and intrinsic values decreasing. *Journal of Management*, *36*(5), 1117–1142. https://doi.org/10.1177/0149206309352246.

Urick, M., Hollensbe, E., Masterson, S., & Lyons, S. (2017). Understanding and managing intergenerational conflict: An examination of influences and strategies. In *Work, aging and retirement* (pp. 166–185). https://doi.org/10.1093/workar/waw009.

HOW TO LEAD TEAMS OF GEN Z EMPLOYEES

Abstract

This chapter offers insights into effective leadership practices for Gen Z teams. It covers various leadership approaches and theories tailored to resonate with the unique characteristics of Generation Z. This chapter outlines a strategic blend of Logoleadership, leadership pedagogy, and SuperLeadership complemented with Self-leadership, each underpinned by the necessity for authenticity, meaningful engagement, and a culture of mutual learning and growth. Additionally, it underscores the critical role of information systems (IS) leadership in harnessing Generation Z's tech-savviness and advocates for team leadership that fosters an inclusive, collaborative environment across generational lines. This comprehensive approach not only aligns with the evolving landscape of leadership criteria, as defined by Generation Z, but also equips leaders with the insights needed to inspire, motivate, and integrate the youngest members of the workforce into the fabric of their organizations effectively.

Kouzes and Posner (2010), which draw on the perspectives of individuals from six continents, tasked participants with identifying the quintessential attributes of leaders they would willingly follow. Four emerged as universally revered out of 25 potential characteristics: honesty, forward-looking, inspiring, and competence. These qualities, which each garnered over 60% of participants' votes, paint a compelling portrait of the modern leader who not only charts a clear path forward but with integrity, inspiration, and adeptness.

DOI: 10.4324/9781032722696-14

Further expanding on this foundation, Kouzes and Posner (2012) articulated five pivotal strategies that elevate a leader's effectiveness in the eyes of their followers. These strategies – Model the Way, Inspire a Shared Vision, Challenge the Process, Enable Others to Act, and Encourage the Heart – offer a practical roadmap for leaders aiming to cultivate a culture of empowerment, innovation, and heartfelt engagement.

LEADERSHIP DEFINED: BY GEN Z

Gen Z employees describe a leader as:

> an individual at a higher hierarchical level, either a boss or a manager, who has a higher status and can do as they please but is also a model of behavior who guides employees. This person takes responsibility, is engaged, and possesses competencies such as planning and realizing ideas. They motivate the team but are also a part of the team.[1]

This cohort, known for its digital nativity and progressive values, delineates leaders not merely by their capacity for autonomous decision-making but also by their hierarchical stature and formal titles. Unlike their predecessors, Millennials and Gen X, Generation Z emphasizes the traditional vestiges of leadership – authority, responsibility, and formal recognition.

For Generation Z, a leader embodies someone who occupies a superior hierarchical position, be it a manager or a boss, endowed with both the privilege of autonomy and the burden of being a behavioral exemplar. This individual not only pioneers vision and strategy – manifested through competencies in planning and realization – but also integrates themselves as a pivotal member of the team. They are characterized by a proactive engagement in their duties and a commitment to motivating the collective, thereby weaving the team's fabric tighter. A tendency towards more individually carrying leaders and emotional intelligence is noticed across the generations.

Navigating the nuances of generational expectations is not just about adapting leadership styles but also about understanding the evolving criteria by which leadership is judged in an era where the lines between formal and informal leadership blur. The insights from Generation Z underscore the enduring importance of recognized leadership roles that come with both the power to act and the responsibility to inspire and integrate.

Leading Generation Z in the workplace requires a nuanced, follower-centric[2] approach spanning leadership theories. This comprehensive strategy combines three primary leadership styles – Logoleadership, Leadership Pedagogy, and SuperLeadership/Self-leadership – with three supplementary ones, forming a robust framework designed to engage and empower the youngest workforce, presented in Table 12.1.

Table 12.1 Leadership Styles for Gen Z-ers

Leadership Theory	Practical Orientation	Source[3]
Multigenerational Leadership	Consideration of multitude of elements ranging from leadership preferences to work values and characteristics of various generational cohorts.	(Dwyer & Azevedo, 2016)
Logoleadership	Active listening, career planning, coaching, mentoring, and training illustrate how employee needs are congruent with organizational needs.	(Mayfield & Mayfield, 2012)
Team leadership	Goal focusing, structuring for results, facilitating decisions, training, maintaining standards, collaborating, managing conflict, and modeling principles.	(Hill, 2016)
Leadership pedagogy	Humble and generous relationships, critical thinking, and expressing consciousness of the learner.	(Freire, 1970)
IS leadership	Adds the dimension of IS to leadership.	(Smaltz et al., 2006)
SuperLeadership	Modeling, encouraging, guiding, and rewarding Self-leadership.	(Manz & Sims, 2001)
Self-leadership	Self-observation, self-goal setting, cue management, self-punishment, self-criticism, rehearsal, and building natural rewards into tasks.	(Manz & Sims, 1991)
Path-goal leadership	Defines goals; clarifies path; removes obstacles for followers; and provides support, clarification, direction, structure, and rewards.	(Dixon & Hart, 2010; R. House, 1971)

LOGOLEADERSHIP: INFUSING MEANING INTO WORK

Central to Logoleadership is the principle that a quest for meaning drives individuals, a concept eloquently mapped out by Frankl (1984) through logotherapy.[4] Leaders can tap into this intrinsic motivation by fostering an environment where Gen Z employees can find profound significance in their roles and contributions. This involves integrating logotherapeutic techniques into daily leadership practices, such as attentive communication, mentorship, planning, career coaching, training, and aligning individual goals with the organization's (Mayfield & Mayfield, 2012). Leaders can help employees navigate their professional journeys by acting as guides and facilitators, ensuring their work resonates with a more profound sense of purpose. Leaders must find meaning in the work and translate it to the employees. Having a clear purpose and internal congruence at all organizational levels improves relationships and engagement (Drucker & Maciariello, 2008; Williams, 1993).

LEADERSHIP PEDAGOGY: FACILITATING LEARNING AND GROWTH

Adopting a pedagogical approach to leadership, as inspired by Freire (1970), transforms the workplace into a dynamic learning environment, especially since Gen Z is in their learning phase in the workplace. Leadership pedagogy creates the conditions for performing pedagogy (Ganz & Lin, 2011). Creating conditions where participants take the initiative to acquire the information, skills, relationships, or other resources they need to achieve a goal encourages learning (Gardner, 1992). This style emphasizes the critical role of education in empowering individuals to challenge and change societal structures. For Gen Z, this translates into creating opportunities that promote self-discovery and the development of critical thinking.

The primary purpose of critical pedagogy is to express experienced employees' consciousness and help them become change agents (McKernan, 2013). Leaders should position themselves as co-learners rather than authoritative figures, encouraging a culture of open dialogue and mutual growth. This pedagogical stance bridges generational divides and prepares Gen Z employees to become change agents within their organizations. The aims of leadership learning are the following five main ones:

1. Express the consciousness of the learners;
2. Recreate knowledge through constant action and reflection;
3. Self-discover and analyze the leader-follower relationship;
4. Practice co-intentional education; and
5. Contradict forms of manipulation leading to domination.

SUPERLEADERSHIP AND SELF-LEADERSHIP: EMPOWERING AUTONOMY

SuperLeadership and Self-leadership revolve around cultivating an organizational culture where individuals are motivated to lead themselves (Manz & Sims, 2001). This approach resonates with Gen Z, a generation known for valuing autonomy and self-direction. By implementing strategies such as initial modeling, guided participation, and gradual Self-leadership development, leaders can encourage Gen Z employees to take ownership of their roles. This empowerment leads to enhanced self-efficacy, innovation, and productivity as employees learn to set goals and devise strategies to achieve them. Self-leadership proposes implementing strategies based on people's thoughts and behaviors to influence themselves (Manz & Sims, 2001). An increased control over the Gen Z follower reduces the follower's sense of self and potential of the individual. Manz and Sims (2001) highlight the following three pillars of Self-leadership theory:

1. **Initial Modeling**: The leader has to demonstrate Self-leadership, and followers are to adopt the standards they observe in the exemplary model;
2. **Guided Participation**: The leader offers followers a safe space to practice Self-leadership; and
3. **Gradual Development of Self-leadership**: The leader shifts the reward pattern toward this process as the follower becomes capable of Self-leadership.

PATH-GOAL THEORY: NAVIGATING THE JOURNEY TO SUCCESS

The Path-Goal Theory complements the primary styles by emphasizing the leader's role in clarifying the path to goal attainment. This involves identifying and removing obstacles and smoothing the way for Gen Z employees to achieve their objectives. Adaptability is critical; leaders must be willing to adjust their leadership style based on the situation and the individual needs of their employees, fostering an environment conducive to continuous learning and growth.

According to the path-goal theory, the leader is responsible for the goal-attainment of followers (Arenas et al., 2017). The leader has to reduce obstacles for followers and make the path towards the objective easier (House, 1971). Effective leadership strategies are contingent on the characteristics of followers, which call for different leadership styles. Depending on the situation, the leader will choose supportive, directive, participative, and achievement-oriented leadership (House & Mitchell, 1974).

INFORMATION SYSTEMS (IS) LEADERSHIP: EMBRACING TECHNOLOGICAL SAVVY

In recognition of Gen Z's affinity for technology, Information Systems (IS) leadership is a crucial style for the digital age. IS leadership requires the extra dimension of IS intelligence to general leadership (Smaltz et al., 2006). This style prioritizes a dual competency in technical knowledge and leadership acumen, aiming to integrate IS within leadership practices strategically. Leaders adept in IS can leverage technology to enhance learning, collaboration, and innovation, thus meeting Gen Z employees' unique needs and expectations.

TEAM LEADERSHIP: FOSTERING COLLABORATIVE EXCELLENCE

Finally, Team Leadership[5] focuses on the dynamic interplay within multigenerational teams. By monitoring and diagnosing team processes, leaders can ensure that the diverse strengths of Gen Z are effectively integrated with those of other generations. This approach enhances team performance and cultivates a culture of inclusivity and mutual respect. When building Gen Z teams, leaders are recommended to contemplate:

- What systems require reorganization through technology?
- What projects require immediate problem-solving through IS or AI?
- Which skills require fast learning?

Box 12.1 Leading Gen Z-ers: Checklist

Drawing from a comprehensive analysis of leadership styles tailored for Gen Z, the following checklist provides actionable insights for business leaders, executives, and managers seeking to foster a dynamic, inclusive, and productive work environment.

Logoleadership: Meaningful Engagement

- ☐ **Identify Personal and Organizational Purpose**: Clearly articulate your meaning in work and communicate how it aligns with organizational goals.
- ☐ **Practice Attentive Communication**: Engage in meaningful dialogues with Gen Z employees, listening to their needs and aspirations.
- ☐ **Foster Mentorship and Coaching**: Establish mentoring programs that connect Gen Z employees with experienced professionals for guidance and growth.
- ☐ **Align Individual and Organizational Goals**: Ensure Gen Z employees understand how their roles contribute to the broader organizational objectives.

Leadership Pedagogy: A Learning Paradigm

- ☐ **Embrace Co-Learning**: Position yourself as a learner alongside Gen Z employees, promoting an environment of mutual growth and discovery.
- ☐ **Encourage Self-discovery**: Create opportunities for Gen Z employees to explore their strengths, interests, and potential career paths.
- ☐ **Foster Critical Thinking**: Challenge Gen Z employees to question, critique, and apply their knowledge to real-world scenarios.

- [ ] **Promote Change Agency**: Support Gen Z employees in identifying and implementing changes that enhance their work and the organization.

SuperLeadership and Self-leadership: Autonomy and Empowerment

- [ ] **Model Self-leadership**: Demonstrate effective self-management strategies that Gen Z employees can emulate.
- [ ] **Provide Safe Spaces for Practice**: Offer projects and tasks that allow Gen Z employees to practice autonomy within a supportive framework.
- [ ] **Facilitate Self-leadership Development**: Gradually transition responsibility and decision-making to Gen Z employees as they demonstrate readiness.

Path-Goal Theory: Clearing the Path to Success**Adapt Leadership Styles**: Flexibly switch between supportive, directive, participative, and achievement-oriented leadership based on the needs of Gen Z employees.

- [ ] **Remove Obstacles**: Actively work to eliminate barriers that hinder Gen Z employees' progress toward their goals.
- [ ] **Facilitate Goal Attainment**: Clearly define objectives and provide the necessary tools and resources for Gen Z employees to achieve them.

IS Leadership: Leveraging Technology

- [ ] **Integrate Technology Strategically**: Utilize digital tools and platforms that resonate with Gen Z's tech-savvy nature to enhance learning and productivity.
- [ ] **Promote Technological Fluency**: Encourage Gen Z employees to develop digital skills to ensure they can effectively navigate the digital aspects of their work.

Team Leadership: Cultivating Collaboration

- [ ] **Diagnose Team Dynamics**: Regularly assess teams' health and productivity, making adjustments as necessary to ensure effective collaboration.
- [ ] **Foster Multigenerational Teams**: Create diverse teams that leverage Gen Z employees' unique strengths and perspectives alongside those of other generations.

CONCLUSIONS

In navigating the intricacies of leading Generation Z in today's dynamic workplace, leaders are called upon to embody a multifaceted approach that harmonizes traditional leadership virtues with innovative strategies that resonate with this digitally native cohort. The synthesis of Logoleadership, leadership pedagogy, SuperLeadership, Self-leadership, and supplementary styles like IS leadership and team leadership provides a robust framework for crafting an engaging and inclusive work environment. This approach is about adapting to Generation Z's unique characteristics and expectations and leveraging their distinct strengths to foster a culture of continuous learning, meaningful engagement, and autonomous innovation. Leaders who skillfully integrate these strategies into their leadership practices are well-positioned to inspire and empower Generation Z employees, enhancing organizational performance and navigating the complexities of the modern business landscape with agility and foresight.

The forward-looking leader recognizes that the essence of effective leadership in the era of Generation Z transcends mere positional authority, embracing instead a holistic view that values authentic engagement, fosters mutual growth, and champions technological savvy. Universal constituents of leadership still run supreme alongside the specific expectations of Generation Z.

Box 12.2 Key Take-Aways for Chapter 12

1 **Initiate Conversations with Purpose**: Develop a habit of engaging in one-on-one conversations with Generation Z employees to uncover and align their ambitions with the organization's broader missions. Utilize these discussions as platforms for mentorship, demonstrating how their daily tasks contribute to meaningful outcomes;

2 **Design Projects as Learning Opportunities**: Whenever assigning projects to Generation Z teams, explicitly frame them as opportunities for growth and learning. Encourage team members to identify learning objectives alongside project goals and facilitate reflection sessions post-completion to consolidate new knowledge and skills;

> 3   **Model and Reward Self-initiative:** Showcase Self-leadership through your actions, making your decision-making processes transparent and your methods for overcoming obstacles visible. Reward Gen Z employees who take initiative, solve problems autonomously, or develop innovative solutions, reinforcing the value of self-directed leadership.

NOTES

1   The quote is a composite summary of the direct words of 30 Gen Z employees asked to describe the term "leader."
2   Followership theories of leadership represents the body of leadership theory that focuses on the followers in contrast to the traditional leadership theories which are leader-centric.
3   The table names the leadership style relevant in leading Gen Z-ers, a brief practical description and indicates sources in the last column for further academic information on the leadership styles presented.
4   See Frankl (1984) for the comprehension of logotheraphy and the role of meaning in work and life.
5   Team leadership is a process-oriented approach in which the leader externalizes and views the group holistically to decide on required interventions. See Hill (2016) for the in-depth explanation of this leadership style.

REFERENCES

Arenas, F. J., Connelly, D., & Williams, M. D. (2017). *Developing your entire range of leadership.* Air University Press.

Dixon, M. L., & Hart, L. (2010). The impact of path-goal leadership styles on work group effectiveness and turnover intention. *Journal of Managerial Issues,* *22*(1), 52–69. https://doi.org/10.2307/25822515.

Drucker, P., & Maciariello, J. (2008). *Management* (J. Collins, Ed.). Harper Collins.

Dwyer, R. J., & Azevedo, A. (2016). Preparing leaders for the multi-generational workforce. *Journal of Enterprising Communities: People and Places in the Global Economy,* *10*(3), 281–305. https://doi.org/10.1108/JEC-08-2013-0025.

Frankl, V. E. (1984). *Man's search for meaning.* Square Press.

Freire, P. (1970). *Pedagogy of the oppressed (M. Ramos, Trans.).* Herder & Herder.

Ganz, M., & Lin, E. (2011). *Learning to lead: Pedagogy of practice. Handbook for teaching leadership: Knowing, doing and being*. Sage.

Gardner, H. (1992). *The unschooled mind*. Basic Books.

Hill, S. (2016). *Team leadership* (P. Northouse, Ed.; Leadership (7th)). Sage Publications.

House, R. (1971). A path goal theory of leader effectiveness. *Administrative Science Quarterly, 16*(3), 321–339. https://doi.org/10.2307/2391905.

House, R. J., & Mitchell, T. R. (1974). Path-goal theory of leadership. *Contemporary Business, 3*, 81–98. https://apps.dtic.mil/dtic/tr/fulltext/u2/a009513.pdf

Kouzes, J., & Posner, B. (2010). *The truth about leadership: The no fads heart of the matter facts you need to know*. Jossey-Bass.

Manz, C., & Sims, H. (1991). SuperLeadership: Beyond the myth of heroic leadership. *Organizational Dynamics, 19*(4), 18–35. https://doi.org/10.1016/0090-2616(91)90051-A

Manz, C., & Sims, H. (2001). *The new superleadership*. Berrett-Koehler.

Mayfield, M., & Mayfield, J. (2012). Logoleadership: Breathing life into loyalty and putting meaning back into work. *Development and Learning in Organizations, 26*(2), 11–15. https://doi.org/10.1108/14777281211201178.

McKernan, J. A. (2013). The origins of critical theory in education: Fabian socialism as social reconstructionism in nineteenth-century Britain. *British Journal of Educational Studies, 61*(4), 417–433. https://www.jstor.org/stable/43896185

Smaltz, D., Sambamurthy, V., & Agarwal, R. (2006). The antecedents of CIO role effectiveness in organizations: An empirical study in the healthcare sector. *IEEE Transactions on Engineering Management, 53*(2), 207–222. https://doi.org/10.1109/TEM.2006.872248.

Williams, L. (1993). *The congruence of people and organizations: Healing dysfunction from the inside out*. Quorum.

HOW TO EMPOWER GEN Z EMPLOYEES

Abstract

This chapter delves into the dynamics of empowerment within the workplace, with a focused lens on Generation Z's unique perspectives and experiences. It explores the intricate power relationships that shape Gen Z's work environment and their perceived levels of empowerment. The narrative is enriched with direct insights from Gen Z individuals, shedding light on their experiences and the specific challenges they face that often lead to feelings of powerlessness. By examining these dynamics, this chapter provides strategic interventions aimed at fostering a more empowered and proactive Gen Z workforce. Through a comprehensive analysis, it offers a blueprint for leaders to enhance empowerment practices, ensuring these align with the aspirations and working styles of the youngest members of the professional world, thus bridging generational gaps and bolstering organizational success.

WHAT IS EMPOWERMENT AT WORK?

Engagement is often discussed regarding employee empowerment (Albrecht & Andreetta, 2011; Laschinger et al., 2009). Empowerment in the workplace is not just a buzzword but a transformative force that shapes how employees engage with their roles and influence their environments. This concept is richly explored through the lens of cognitive empowerment, a model developed by Thomas and Velthouse (1990). This model posits that employee behavior and decisions are driven by cognitive assessments that extend beyond

DOI: 10.4324/9781032722696-15

the tangible and observable. According to their seminal work, empowerment is fundamentally about altering cognitive variables or task assessments that fuel employee motivation (Thomas & Velthouse, 1990).

Moving away from an objectivist standpoint, which limits cognition to externally verifiable realities, the constructivist approach offers a broader canvas. It enriches the perception of facts by infusing them with more profound meaning and relevance (Thomas & Velthouse, 1990). This model identifies four vital psychological dimensions critical to fostering empowerment: meaningfulness, impact, competence, and choice. These elements are theoretical constructs and actionable insights that can guide leaders in crafting a work environment where empowerment is a buzzword and a palpable driving force. By nurturing these dimensions, leaders can create a workplace where employees feel genuinely motivated, valued, and confident in their ability to make decisions and effect change. Below is a breakdown of each:

- **Meaningfulness**: Meaningfulness refers to the significance and value an employee attaches to their work based on their ideals and standards. When perceived as meaningful, it aligns with what matters personally to the employee. This could be because the work taps into their passions, feels ethically rewarding, or contributes to a more significant cause. Employers can enhance meaningfulness by connecting day-to-day activities to the organization's mission or demonstrating how individual roles contribute to broader societal impacts.
- **Impact**: Impact is about the influence an employee believes they have within the organization. It is the perception that their actions lead to noticeable outcomes and that they are an effective agent of change within their sphere of influence. When employees see that their work makes a difference, their sense of empowerment increases. Leaders can foster a sense of impact by providing clear feedback on how employees' work results in positive changes and by celebrating successes that directly result from employees' efforts.
- **Competence**: Competence refers to an employee's belief in their ability to perform job tasks successfully. This dimension is bolstered through professional development, positive feedback, and assignments that challenge employees within the realm of

their skills and slightly beyond. As employees grow more skilled and knowledgeable, their confidence in their capabilities increases, reinforcing their sense of competence.

- **Choice**: Choice involves employees having the autonomy to decide their work processes, methods, and tasks. It is the freedom to approach tasks in ways they determine best. Autonomy is a critical factor in job satisfaction and organizational commitment. Empowering employees with choice can mean decentralizing decision-making, reducing micromanagement, and encouraging a culture where ideas and suggestions from all levels are valued and explored.

THE LAY OF THE BUSINESS LANDSCAPE ON EMPOWERMENT: MANAGERS' VIEWPOINT

The data reveal that while managers believe they are employing various techniques to foster empowerment, a notable gap exists in their engagement with the concept. Many managers do not consider or strategically integrate empowerment into their leadership practices. There is no standard for empowering recruits, integrating them, or measuring their level of engagement.

Further examination shows that the recruitment process is well-aligned with the principles of empowerment, suggesting that initial engagement efforts should be strong. In other words, it's essential to empower from the start of the onboarding process – which, if it happens, is undoubtedly not managed.

Further, technology's influence emerges as a double-edged sword; either it can significantly enhance empowerment by providing tools that foster autonomy and efficiency or it can become a source of disempowerment if it leads to increased monitoring or reduces employees' agency in their daily tasks.

For leaders aiming to bridge these gaps, a strategic reevaluation of how empowerment is defined and implemented at all stages of employee interaction is crucial. Enhancing awareness among management teams about the practical implications of empowerment – and the tools they employ to achieve it – will be essential. Additionally, integrating technology in ways that promote rather than inhibit employee autonomy will be essential for fostering an environment where empowerment is not just a policy but a palpable part of the organizational culture. This approach ensures that the initial promise of empowerment during recruitment extends throughout an employee's tenure, enhancing engagement, satisfaction, and productivity (Table 13.1).

Table 13.1 The Lay of the Business Landscape. Integration, Empowerment, and Engagement Evaluation

Empowerment Category	*Summary of Manager Responses*
Process of integrating a young employee	Integrating a young employee can be either a standardized or an intuitive, personalized process that may entail a probation period. The predominant focus is on competence; the young employees have a mentor or an experienced employee to guide them. Role, expectations, rights/obligations, and workflow are explained. Also, the young employee may receive materials and undertake specialized courses. The company creates support and safety, and small firms treat young employees like family. However, it is also the choice of the employee to integrate and to decide if the company is the right fit and if they like the work.
Methods of empowerment	Employees are empowered through financial rewards, verbal appreciation, managerial support, and skills training. Their ideas can be integrated, and they can be involved in the technologicalization process. They have decision-making power, their creativity is encouraged, and they are shown trust is placed in them. Some managers highlight the common good and the beautiful parts of the work.
Evaluation of employee engagement	Employee engagement is evaluated predominantly through results and achievements. Reviews, reports, evaluations, and homework are tracked. Various behaviors are monitored, such as collaboration, punctuality, and doing more than expected. Engagement is also evaluated in terms of loyalty, reliability, and the employee's enjoyment of work. Process-wise, there is no formalized standard for evaluation; it is an informal process, often with daily check-ins. The HR department may be responsible.

WHY DO GEN Z-ERS FEEL DISEMPOWERED?

The insights from the research on power dynamics offer a nuanced understanding of why Generation Z employees might feel disempowered at work. This group often grapples with feelings of inferiority and a strong desire for recognition, aligning with Adler (1927) theory, which posits that human striving for superiority stems from an innate sense of inferiority, met with grandiosity, eagerness, and sometimes rebelliousness. These psychological dynamics are reflected in some of the less desirable behaviors exhibited by Generation Z in the workplace.

Further compounding this issue, employees across age groups may carry unresolved personal dynamics into the workplace, a phenomenon known as transference (Bernstein, 2013). This can manifest as senior employees perceiving the integration of a young worker similarly to adopting a child, fostering a dynamic where the younger employee feels helpless and dependent, thus reinforcing a cycle of disempowerment. In the workspace, the young employee, as in a family, may feel helpless and incapable (Adler, 1927). Thus, it would be the role of the older employee to lead the inexperienced Generation Z employee towards self-actualization – that is, maturation.

Moreover, the entrenched power structures within organizations often see tenured employees – typically from older generations such as Boomers or Gen X – dominating leadership roles and decision-making processes, thus setting the terms of engagement and advancement. In this hierarchy, young employees, primarily from Generations Y and Z, find themselves at the lower end of the power spectrum, frequently feeling overlooked and undervalued. Their main avenue for asserting influence is gaining prestige and recognition, which, if not provided, often leads to job turnover as a last resort for asserting control.

On the managerial front, there is a notable disconnect between integrating young employees and the broader engagement strategies within companies. Managers focus on integrating Gen Z employees by creating competence and offering choices. They often overlook the crucial aspect of impact, leading to incomplete empowerment (Heimburger et al., 2020). Engagement evaluations, which are heavily results-oriented and lack a standardized approach, fail to enhance engagement meaningfully (Harter, 2017; Mann & Harter, 2016).

Checklist: 5 Actions Managers Can Take to Empower Young Recruits

✓ **Tech-Savvy Onboarding – Integrating Gen Z into the Digital Workplace**: Given Generation Z's innate comfort with technology, managers should integrate advanced digital tools for day-to-day operations and training and development. Employ interactive and tech-forward platforms for onboarding sessions and encourage collaboration tools that allow young recruits to work effectively from any location. This meets their technological expectations and enhances their productivity and engagement.

✓ **Guiding the Next Gen – How to Build a Robust Mentorship Program for Young Talent**: Pair each young recruit with a more experienced mentor within the company. This relationship should be structured to offer guidance, feedback, and support, focusing on professional growth and skill development. Ensure that mentors are trained to be directive yet supportive, aligning with Gen Z's preference for authoritative and nurturing leaders (Lancaster & Stillman, 2003).

✓ **Empower with Purpose – Giving Gen Z the Keys to the Kingdom**: Empower young recruits by giving them ownership of projects within clear boundaries. This builds their confidence and competence while satisfying their need for direction and structure. Start with small, manageable projects and increase their complexity as the recruits demonstrate readiness and capability, fostering a sense of accomplishment and belonging.

✓ **Feedback Is Fuel – Cultivating a Culture of Continuous Improvement for Gen Z**: Implement a continuous, constructive feedback and recognition system. Gen Z values immediate and ongoing feedback that helps them understand their performance and areas for improvement. Complement this with public acknowledgment of their successes to boost morale and motivation.

✓ **Tailored Trajectories – Customizing Career Paths for Young Innovators**: Recognize each young recruit's interests and career aspirations. Tailor development opportunities that align with their personal and professional goals, such as specialized training in desired skills or involvement in projects that pique their interest. This personalized approach increases job satisfaction and aids in retention as employees feel their specific needs and contributions are valued.

CONCLUSIONS

In an era where dynamic workplace environments are the norm, understanding and enhancing empowerment for Generation Z is beneficial and imperative for sustained organizational success. Managers need to cultivate an environment where young employees are heard and actively involved in shaping their roles and responsibilities. This involves embracing a model where empowerment goes beyond mere engagement, encouraging Gen Z to take initiative and make decisions that influence actual outcomes. Organizations can unlock a powerful source of innovation and drive by fostering a workplace that values autonomy and acknowledges the unique contributions of younger team members.

Leadership needs to address the nuanced needs of Generation Z by integrating empowerment strategies that span technological integration, mentorship, and personalized development plans. By doing so, organizations will mitigate the challenges associated with feelings of disempowerment among young employees and enhance their overall engagement and productivity. These strategies must be executed with a clear understanding of their impact on the younger workforce, ensuring that the efforts to empower genuinely resonate with and support Generation Z employees' professional growth and satisfaction.

To effectively empower Generation Z, managers must embrace and integrate all dimensions of empowerment – choice, competence, impact, and meaningfulness – into their management practices. Additionally, involving Gen Z employees in key processes such as technologization can significantly boost their sense of agency and belonging, aligning their personal growth with organizational success.

Box 13.1 Critical Take-Aways for Chapter 13

1   **Deploy Tech-Enhanced Onboarding:** Utilize cutting-edge technology to streamline onboarding and daily operations, catering to Gen Z's digital fluency and expectations for a modern workplace;

2   **Establish Structured Mentorship**: Create robust mentorship programs that pair young employees with experienced mentors, fostering an environment of guidance and continuous professional growth;
3   **Grant Project Ownership**: Empower Gen Z employees by assigning them ownership of projects within defined limits. This will enhance their skills and boost their confidence through hands-on experience.

REFERENCES

Adler, A. (1927). Individual psychology. *The Journal of Abnormal and Social Psychology*, *22*(2), 116–122. https://doi.org/10.1037/h0072190.

Albrecht, S. L., & Andreetta, M. (2011). The influence of empowering leadership, empowerment and engagement on affective commitment and turnover intentions in community health service workers: Test of a model. *Leadership in Health Services*, *24*(3), 1751–1879. https://doi.org/10.1108/17511871 111151126.

Bernstein, S. D. (2013). Detecting and responding constructively to transference in the workplace. *Journal of Management & Organization*, *19*(1), 75–85. https://doi.org/10.1017/jmo.2013.5.

Harter, J. (2017). *Dismal employee engagement is a sign of global mismanagement.* https://www.gallup.com/workplace/231668/dismal-employee-engagement-sign-global-mismanagement.aspx

Heimburger, L., Buchweitz, L., Gouveia, R., & Korn, O. (2020). Gamifying onboarding: How to increase both engagement and integration of new employees. In R. H. M. Goossens & A. Murata (Eds.), *Advances in social and occupational ergonomics* (pp. 3–14). Springer International Publishing. https://doi.org/10.1007/978-3-030-20145-6_1.

Lancaster, L. C., & Stillman, D. (2003). *When generations collide: Who they are.* Collins.

Laschinger, H., Wilk, P., & Cho, J. (2009). Empowerment, engagement and perceived effectiveness in nursing work environments: Does experience matter? *Journal of Nursing Management*, *17*(5), 636–646. https://doi.org/10.1111/j.1365-2834.2008.00907.x.

Mann, A., & Harter, J. (2016). *The worldwide employee engagement crisis*. Gallup. https://static1.squarespace.com/static/552b3ee0e4b016252ff74ac0/t/ 59b652928dd04187fcfd085a/1505120914868/The+Worldwide+ Employee+Engagement+Crisis+Gallup.pdf

Thomas, K. W., & Velthouse, B. A. (1990). Cognitive elements of empower- ment: An "interpretive" model of intrinsic task motivation. *The Academy of Management Review*, *15*(4), 666–681. https://doi.org/10.2307/258687.

WHAT TO DO ABOUT 'QUIET QUITTING'?

Abstract

This chapter investigates the 'quiet quitting' phenomenon among Generation Z in the workplace and unveils the Employee Lifecycle Curve. It explores the multifaceted strategies that define quitting and proposes actionable insights for leaders to engage and retain this dynamic segment of the workforce effectively. By identifying key behaviors and trends – such as the dip in discretionary effort, changes in team dynamics and communication patterns, and a decrease in the quality of work – leaders can preemptively address signs of 'quiet quitting.' Furthermore, this chapter illuminates the Gen Z employee lifecycle, emphasizing the critical junctures for intervention to maintain engagement and prolong tenure. It provides insights into the types and phases of quiet quitters and strategies to mitigate this disengagement through rapid integration. Through the lens of the Exit, Voice, Loyalty, Neglect (EVLN) model, the discussion expands to encompass the broader implications of employee responses to job dissatisfaction, offering an understanding to leaders of the dynamics that characterize workforces.

WHAT IS 'QUIET QUITTING'?[1]

A silent but profound transformation is underway, which demands urgent attention from every forward-thinking leader: 'quiet quitting.' This phenomenon, increasingly prevalent among Generation

DOI: 10.4324/9781032722696-16

Z employees, heralds a seismic shift in workplace engagement, signaling a disengagement wave that has washed over more than half of the global workforce (Smith, 2022), and continues to ripple outward with increasing momentum (McGregor, 2022).

Interestingly, the concept of 'quiet quitting' may not be entirely new but has been reframed for today's context. 'Quiet quitting' emerges not merely as a passive response but as a nuanced strategy undertaken by employees to assert boundaries, protect their well-being, and navigate the complexities of modern work cultures (Hare, 2022).

Mark Bolger coined 'quiet quitting' from the digital echo chambers of social media (Buscaglia, 2022) and has since morphed into a rallying cry for a reimagined workplace ethos (Ellis & Yang, 2022). This evolving concept blurs the lines between mere disengagement and a strategic withdrawal of discretionary effort – where employees no longer aspire to exceed expectations or contribute beyond their basic job descriptions (Hetler, 2022; Mahand & Caldwell, 2023). This shift towards minimalism in work effort spawns a complex debate, with scholars divided over its interpretation: some view it as a detrimental trend, while others argue it is a legitimate counter-response to escalating workplace demands (Hopke, 2022).

Managers' discourse around 'quiet quitting' is as varied as it is vibrant. Critics express concern over its psychological toll (Hetler, 2022), while some economists speculate on its self-regulating potential amidst changing market dynamics (Johnson, 2023). The backdrop of the COVID-19 pandemic provides context to the reduced working hours, hinting at a broader societal and economic recalibration. The business response calls for a fundamental overhaul of HR practices and reconstitution of the psychological contract between employers and employees, steering toward more meaningful engagement (Klotz & Bolino, 2022; Zenger & Folkman, 2022).

Box 14.1 Audit to Detect 'Quiet Quitting' among Gen Z Employees

Conduct a precise, actionable audit to uncover the signs of 'quiet quitting':

- ☐ **Dip in Discretionary Effort:** Look for signs like a lack of initiative, decreased willingness to take on additional responsibilities, or a sudden disinterest in participating in projects beyond their job descriptions.
- ☐ **Reduced Engagement in Team Dynamics:** A shift from active participation to silence in meetings, reluctance to share ideas, or a noticeable decrease in collaboration with peers can indicate disengagement. This detachment from the group's dynamics is often a precursor to 'quiet quitting,' signaling a withdrawal from their tasks and the organizational culture itself. It may also include an increase in absenteeism and lateness.
- ☐ **Shift in Communication Patterns:** They send shorter, less enthusiastic emails, a decrease in proactive communications, or a reluctance to engage in face-to-face interactions.
- ☐ **Decline in Quality and Creativity of Work:** This might look like doing the bare minimum on assignments, a lack of enthusiasm for creative problem-solving, or an overall drop in the attention to detail that used to characterize their work.

This five-point audit is designed to diagnose and prompt early intervention if deemed valuable and necessary.

THE GEN Z EMPLOYEE LIFECYCLE

Gen Z's entrance into the workforce dramatically reconfigures the employee lifecycle, which now averages a mere year – a stark contrast to the multi-decade tenures of their Boomer predecessors (Fry, 2019). A series of engagement ebbs punctuate this transient tenure of Generation Z and flows, culminating more often than not in this gradual disengagement known as 'quiet quitting.'

To navigate this new terrain, it is imperative to understand the engagement typologies of Generation Z employees.[2] These range from Activists – vibrantly engaged and invested in their work – to Isolates, who are disenchanted and disengaged. Between these extremes lie Diehards with their steadfast commitment, Participants actively engaged yet flexible, and Bystanders who maintain a neutral stance despite their engagement.

The lifecycle of a Generation Z employee within a single year is marked by predictable shifts in behavior, initially bursting onto the scene as Activists, full of zeal but lacking in-depth knowledge. This enthusiasm propels them towards a peak of dedication as they oscillate between Activists and Participants in the first few months. However, by the mid-year mark, a slide towards Bystander status begins, with 'quiet quitting' typically setting in between the seventh and eighth month. By the mid-year mark, employees are often already seeking different opportunities. Attempts by employers to counter this shift – through interventions like job redesign, bonuses, and flexible working arrangements – often fall short of rekindling the initial Activist fervor or significantly extending their stay. However, by the end of the 12th month, they often reach the point of isolation, accompanied by requests for a raise to adjust their engagement levels for the subsequent period. Despite efforts to address 'quiet quitting' through interventions like workload redistribution, job redesign, bonuses, and flexible work practices, these measures have proven ineffective in significantly altering the employee lifecycle.

This pattern of engagement, with its distinct phases and rapid transitions, suggests a critical window for managerial intervention: the early activist and diehard stages. During these phases, strategic efforts to deepen organizational integration and prolong the participant phase could yield substantial dividends. In other words, managers should take advantage of an improved onboarding and rapid integration system to fully benefit from the proactive period of Gen Z engagement.

Box 14.2 Primer on the Exit, Voice, Loyalty, Neglect (EVLN) Model

At its core, the EVLN framework identifies four cardinal reactions – Exit, Voice, Loyalty, and Neglect – each representing a unique navigational path employees might choose to reconcile with diminishing job fulfillment.[3] Leaders will hear 'quiet quitting,' often discussed within the extended EVLN model's lenses.[4] Neglect, silence, and workplace incivility introduce nuances like withholding critical information as a form of disengagement.

1   **Exit:** This response is characterized by a physical departure from the organization, be it through resignation, job transfer, or even the contemplation of such actions (Allen & Tuselmann, 2009;

McShane et al., 2009; Rusbult et al., 1986; Todor, 1980). It represents a definitive break, a tangible severance from the source of dissatisfaction.

2   **Voice**: In stark contrast, Voice embodies the proactive pursuit of change. It is the choice to face issues head-on, advocating for transformation through feedback, dialogue, or creative problem-solving rather than exist (Allen, 2014; Turnley & Feldman, 1999). This route signals a commitment to improvement, leveraging voice for positive change.

3   **Loyalty**: Loyalty epitomizes patience and faith in the organization's capacity for self-correction and growth. It is a passive but hopeful stance, where employees, despite their grievances, choose to stand by their employer, anticipating future betterment (McShane et al., 2009; Rusbult et al., 1986). This approach underscores a deep-seated allegiance and optimism.

4   **Neglect**: Mirroring Exit in its destructive nature; Neglect reflects an internal withdrawal marked by diminished effort, increased absenteeism, and a general lapse in performance standards (Hagedoorn et al., 1999; Rusbult et al., 1986). It is a silent retreat from engagement and responsibility.

The interplay between employee responses and the quality of leader-member relationships underscores a significant correlation: Employees who perceive a high-quality connection with their leaders are more inclined towards Voice and Loyalty, eschewing Exit and Neglect even when faced with workplace injustices (Lee & Varon, 2020). This insight, particularly relevant for the older generational groups, is less salient among Generation Z employees, who champion the 'quiet quitting' movement and become less attached even to the highest connection to leaders.

THE 'QUIET QUITTING' CURVE

Figure 14.1 illustrates behavioral shifts in Generation Z employees occurring approximately every three months within this one year.[5] 'Quiet quitting' among Generation Z employees manifests through a triad of reveling strategies. These tactics – ego-oriented, image-oriented, and achievement-oriented[6] – aligns with the expanded dimensions of the EVLN model, precisely the facets of silence and

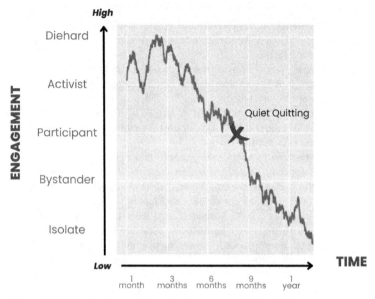

Figure 14.1 The Employee Lifecycle Curve from Ochis (2024).

neglect, offering a compelling lens through which to view modern employee behavior.

Ego-Oriented Strategies: At the core of the ego-oriented approach lies a strategic retreat, a calculated withdrawal to safeguard personal interests and well-being. This method underscores a prioritization of self, where disengagement protects against workplace demands that might threaten personal boundaries or health.

Image-Oriented Strategies: The image-oriented tactic is a masterclass in visibility management. Employees adept at this strategy curate their presence to be most notable in the eye of leadership, engaging in a selective display of commitment that ensures their efforts are recognized, yet only when it guarantees maximum visibility. This approach cleverly navigates the fine line between perceived engagement and personal energy conservation.

Achievement-Oriented Strategies: The achievement-oriented pathway champions record every detail of one's workload and inform the superior of every action undertaken to highlight the high level of performance and value added to the company. This tactic is used to leverage the relationship with the superior.

CONCLUSIONS

The stark realities of managing Generation Z in the workplace call for a different approach to employee engagement. Current organizational practices lack a cohesive employee integration system, resulting in disjointed interventions. Managerial efforts to counter the 'quiet quitting' phase have shown limited effectiveness in extending employee tenure. A more resource-efficient strategy entails improving onboarding and integration practices to extend the participant phase of Generation Z employees while leveraging their enthusiasm during the activist and diehard phases. Focusing on these early stages of employment can delay the onset of 'quiet quitting' and forge a more enduring and mutually beneficial relationship between Generation Z employees and their organizations.

Box 14.3 Critical Take-Aways for Chapter 14

1 **Prioritize Early Engagement**: Harness Generation Z employees' initial activist and diehard phases with improved onboarding and rapid integration systems. The initial months are golden – capitalize on this period of high enthusiasm and commitment to embed these young professionals deeply into your organizational fabric. Early, meaningful engagement is critical to extending their tenure beyond the average one-year lifecycle;

2 **Monitor Behavioral Shifts**: Stay vigilant for signs of 'quiet quitting' among your Gen Z workforce by conducting regular audits on discretionary effort, team dynamics, communication patterns, work quality, and attendance. Observing these indicators can provide early warnings, allowing for timely interventions that could reinvigorate engagement and commitment;

3 **Understand the EVLN Framework**: Familiarize yourself with the Exit, Voice, Loyalty, Neglect (EVLN) model to better comprehend the spectrum of employee reactions to dissatisfaction.

Recognizing where your Gen Z employees fall within these categories can guide more strategic, tailored responses to foster a more fulfilling work environment.

NOTES

1   See Ochis (2024) for comprehensive research on 'quiet quitting'.
2   The typologies utilized are Kellerman's follower typology (2008).
3   Originally introduced by Hirschman (1970) and subsequently refined by thought leaders such as Rusbult et al. (1982) and Farrell (1983), this model delineates the spectrum of responses employees may exhibit as their job satisfaction wanes.
4   Naus et al. (2007) contend that if certain behaviors are absent from the EVLN model's suggested alternatives, additional responses can be introduced by extending the original model.
5   For a comprehensive description of the Employee Lifecycle Curve, see Ochis (2024).
6   Gen Z's strategies mirror the approaches Millennials have adopted to navigate the complexities of intergenerational workplace dynamics with the Boomer generation. See the research of Urick et al. (2017).

REFERENCES

Allen, M., & Tuselmann, H. (2009). All powerful voice? The need to include "exit", "loyalty" and "neglect" in empirical studies too. *Employee Relations*, *31*, 538–552. https://doi.org/10.1108/01425450910979275.

Allen, M. M. C. (2014). Hirschman and voice. In A. Wilkinson, J. Donaghey, T. Dundon, & R. B. Freeman (Eds.), *Handbook of research on employee voice*. Edward Elgar Publishing. https://doi.org/10.4337/9780857939272.00010.

Buscaglia, M. (2022). A quick look at the origins and outcomes of the trendy term. *Chicago Tribune*. Available at: PressReader.Com - Digital Newspaper & Magazine Subscriptions.

Ellis, L., & Yang, A. (2022, August 25). *What is quiet quitting? Employees set boundaries for better work-life balance.* MarketWatch. https://www.marketwatch.com/story/meet-the-so-called-quiet-quitters-i-still-get-just-as-much-accomplished-i-just-dont-stress-and-internally-rip-myself-to-shreds-11661372447

Farrell, D. (1983). Exit, voice, loyalty, and neglect as responses to job dissatisfaction: A multidimensional scaling study. *Academy of Management Journal*, *26*(4), 596–607. https://doi.org/10.5465/255909

Fry, R. (2019). *Baby Boomers are staying in the labor force at rates not seen in generations for people their age*. Pew Research Center. https://www.pewresearch.org/short-reads/2019/07/24/baby-boomers-us-labor-force/

Hagedoorn, M., Van Yperen, N. W., Van De Vliert, E., & Buunk, B. P. (1999). Employees' reactions to problematic events: A circumplex structure of five categories of responses, and the role of job satisfaction. *Journal of Organizational Behavior*, *20*(3), 309–321. https://doi.org/10.1002/(SICI)1099-1379 (199905)20:3<309::AID-JOB895>3.0.CO;2–P

Hare, N. (2022). What Is 'Quiet Quitting' and how should leaders respond? Forbes. https://www.forbes.com/sites/allbusiness/2022/09/01/what-is-quiet-quitting-and-how-should-leaders-respond/?sh=6636d74e6de0

Hetler, A. (2022). Quiet quitting explained: Everything you need to know. *Whatis.Com*. https://www.techtarget.com/whatis/feature/Quiet-quitting-explained-Everything-you-need-to-know.

Hirschman, A. O. (2004). *Exit, voice, and loyalty: Responses to decline in firms, organizations, and states*. Harvard University Press.

Hopke, T. (2022). The culture reset gift most companies needed. *Forbes*. https://www.forbes.com/sites/teresahopke/2022/09/30/quiet-quittingthe-culture-resetgift-most-companies-needed/

Johnson, J. R. (2023). What's new about quiet quitting (and what's not). *The Transdisciplinary Journal of Management*. https://tjm.scholasticahq.com/article/72079-what-s-new-about-quiet-quitting-and-what-s-not

Klotz, A. C., & Bolino, M. C. (2022). When quiet quitting is worse than the real thing. *Harvard Business Review*. https://hbr.org/2022/09/when-quiet-quitting-is-worse-than-the-real-thing

Lee, J., & Varon, A. L. (2020). Employee Exit, Voice, Loyalty, and Neglect in Response to Dissatisfying Organizational Situations: It Depends on Supervisory Relationship Quality. *International Journal of Business Communication (Thousand Oaks, Calif.)*, *57*(1), 30–51. https://doi.org/10.1177/2329488416675839

Mahand, T., & Caldwell, C. (2023). Quiet quitting: Causes and opportunities. *Business and Management Research*, *12*(1), 9–19. https://doi.org/10.5430/bmr.v12n1p9.

McGregor, G. (2022). *Before "quiet quitting" in the U.S., there was "lying flat" in China. How the anti-work movement swept the world's two largest economies*.

https://search.ebscohost.com/login.aspx?direct=true&db=bsu&AN=1588
81425&lang=tr

McShane, S. L., Olekalns, M., & Travaglione, T. (2009). *Organisational behaviour on the pacific rim*. McGraw-Hill.

Naus, F., van Iterson, A., & Roe, R. (2007). Organizational cynicism: Extending the Exit, Voice, Loyalty, and Neglect Model of employees' responses to adverse conditions in the workplace. *Human Relations, 60*(5), 683–718. https://doi.org/10.1177/0018726707079198

Ochis, K. (2024). Generation Z and "quiet quitting": Rethinking onboarding in an era of employee disengagement. *Multidisciplinary Business Review, 17*(1), 83–97. https://doi.org/10.35692/07183992.17.1.7.

Rusbult, C. E., Johnson, D. J., & Morrow, G. D. (1986). Determinants and consequences of exit, voice, loyalty, and neglect: Responses to dissatisfaction in adult romantic involvements. *Human Relations, 39*(1), 45–63. https://doi.org/10.1177/001872678603900103.

Smith, R. A. (2022). Quiet quitters make up half the U.S workforce, gallup says. *Wall Street Journal*. https://www.wsj.com/articles/quiet-quitters-make-up-half-the-u-s-workforce-gallup-says-11662517806

Todor, M. D. (1980). *A movement paradox: Turnover? Transfer? Annual Meetings of the Academy of Management*, Detroit, MI.

Turnley, W. H., & Feldman, D. C. (1999). The impact of psychological contract violations on exit, voice, loyalty, and neglect. *Human Relations, 52*(7), 895–922. https://doi.org/10.1177/001872679905200703.

Urick, M., Hollensbe, E., Masterson, S., & Lyons, S. (2017). Understanding and managing intergenerational conflict: An examination of influences and strategies. In *Work, Aging And Retirement* (pp. 166–185). https://doi.org/10.1093/workar/waw009.

Zenger, J., & Folkman, J. (2022). Quiet quitting is about bad bosses, not bad employees. *Harvard Business Review*. https://hbr.org/2022/08/quiet-quitting-is-about-bad-bosses-not-bademployees

PART III

TOOLKIT FOR TRANSFORMATION – SHORT GUIDES FOR IMPLEMENTATION

HOW TO MAKE DIFFERENT GENERATIONS OF EMPLOYEES WORK TOGETHER

Abstract

This chapter focuses on actionable techniques for fostering collaboration among diverse age groups within organizations. It begins with essential guidance on forming effective multi-generational teams, emphasizing the value of diversity in team composition. This chapter progresses to strategic task assignments based on individual capabilities and concludes with insights on selecting the right leaders for multigenerational teams. This chapter introduces the ACORN business model as a comprehensive framework to enhance workplace inclusivity and productivity by accommodating employee differences, creating flexible workplace options, and respecting the competence and initiative of all staff members. Additionally, it explores actionable techniques for building and managing teams that bridge generational gaps and align these diverse talents toward achieving common organizational objectives, ultimately boosting engagement and driving innovative team performance. The synthesis here offers leaders a blueprint for transforming generational diversity from a potential obstacle to a formidable organizational asset.

MAXIMIZING TEAM POTENTIAL: HOW TO BUILD MULTIGENERATION TEAMS?

In today's dynamic workplace, leveraging generational diversity is not just about recognizing differences but strategically utilizing these differences to fortify the organization's performance. Kupperschmidt

DOI: 10.4324/9781032722696-18

(2006) emphasizes that understanding and harnessing these variances can significantly enhance employee productivity, spur innovation, and strengthen corporate citizenship. Managers play a crucial role in this process by skillfully constructing multigenerational teams. To optimize team composition, managers should consider specific dynamics and questions, as outlined in Table 15.1, that guide the selection of team leaders and members based on their generational strengths and perspectives.

Table 15.1 Source: Questions to Ask When Building Mixed Generation Teams

Generational Cohort	Questions
Questions to ask Boomers to value and use their strengths	1. Where can we most effectively use team members with strengths in mentoring? 2. Which issues require consensus building? 3. Which issues require a process orientation?
Questions to ask Generation X to value and use their strengths	1. Which jobs call for an entrepreneurial spirit? 2. Where do we need technologically skilled colleagues? 3. How can trouble-shooting skills be more effectively valued and used?
Questions to ask Generation Y to value and use their strengths	1. How can we best value and use culturally sensitive viewpoints? 2. How can we best incorporate new technology skills? 3. How can colleagues become comfortable and competent within a virtual team?
Questions to ask Generation Z to value and use their strengths	1. How can we best integrate LGBTQ-sensitive perspectives? 2. Which processes need to be revamped entirely? 3. Which tasks require self-study through the Internet? 4. How can AI be integrated into processes? 5. Which tasks can be automated through machine learning?

Source: Adapted from Kupperschmidt, B. (2006) for the first three generations. Completed by author.

Generation X is often seen as uniquely positioned to lead these diverse teams. With a broad understanding of the values and expectations of both Boomers and Millennials, Gen X leaders can bridge generational gaps, facilitating a more prosperous collaboration that capitalizes on each cohort's distinct capabilities.

Nevertheless, after building the teams, this approach requires a model of collaboration, where the focus is on aligning diverse generational talents and insights toward shared organizational goals. By doing so, businesses can increase engagement across all age groups and drive more coherent and innovative team performance.

ACORN BUSINESS MODEL FOR MANAGING GENERATIONS[1]

Kupperschmidt (2000) proposed the ACORN business model, which provides a robust framework for fostering an inclusive and productive workplace environment. Each element of the model outlines strategic actions that leaders can adopt to manage generational diversity effectively:

1. **Accommodating Employee Differences**: Embracing diversity within the workforce is fundamental. This involves understanding and valuing each employee's distinct backgrounds, skills, and perspectives. Leaders should foster an environment where these differences are acknowledged and seen as assets that enhance team creativity and problem-solving capabilities. Tailoring communication and management approaches to fit diverse employee needs is a critical step in this process.

2. **Creating Workplace Choices**: Flexibility is key in attracting and retaining top talent across all generations. This aspect of the ACORN model advocates for providing employees with choices that cater to their varying work style preferences, life stages, and career aspirations. Whether it is flexible hours, telecommuting options, or customized career paths, offering choices empowers employees to work in ways that best suit their productivity and well-being.

3. **Operating from a Theoretically Sound, Sophisticated Management Style**: Today's leaders must be well-versed in both traditional management theories and contemporary

leadership practices. A sophisticated management style informed by empirical research and best practices enables managers to navigate the complexities of a diverse workforce. This involves continuous learning and adapting management strategies to ensure they are adequate across different generational needs and expectations.

4. **Respecting Employees' Competence and Initiative**: Recognition and respect for each employee's skills and contributions are crucial. This principle of the ACORN model emphasizes the importance of trusting employees to take initiative and make decisions. By delegating meaningful responsibilities and providing the necessary support, leaders can foster a sense of ownership and accountability among employees. Respecting their competence increases motivation and engagement, driving individual and organizational success.

5. **Nourishing Retention**: Retaining skilled employees is more cost-effective than acquiring new talent. Nourishing retention involves creating a supportive and engaging work environment that encourages employees to stay and grow with the company. This includes providing competitive compensation, benefits, professional development opportunities, and a positive workplace culture that aligns with their values and career goals.

By implementing the ACORN model, organizations can develop a strategic approach to generational management that addresses the challenges and leverages the diverse strengths of their workforce. This holistic view fosters a collaborative, dynamic, resilient organizational culture poised for long-term success.

MAXIMIZING TEAM POTENTIAL: HARNESSING GENERATIONAL DIVERSITY THROUGH CAREFRONTING

In a workplace where generational differences often lead to conflict, adopting a carefronting approach can transform these challenges into opportunities for growth and collaboration. Carefronting prioritizes the maintenance of effective, productive working relationships through a method of communication that combines self-care with the courage to confront issues directly and responsibly. Ausburger's

(1973) model of carefronting is based on communication to manage intergenerational workplace conflict effectively and manage multiple generations. Ausberger (1973, 1981) proposed the model of carefronting for family therapy, namely caring enough to confront. Carefronting is based on the following pillars:

1. The parties involved in conflict must be willing and able to state how they feel and what they value;
2. I-statements ought to be utilized;
3. The negotiation of differences is carried out in a transparent, respectful, and truthful way (Augsburger, 1973); and
4. Forgiveness is essential for all parties involved (Augsburger, 1981).

In Practice, This Technique Emphasizes Several Actionable Strategies:

- **Practice Truthing**: Leaders must foster an environment where multiple perspectives are acknowledged and valued. This involves listening with empathy and expressing one's viewpoints honestly to build mutual understanding.
- **Own and Manage Anger**: Recognize that anger is a natural conflict response, but managing how it is expressed is vital. Leaders should encourage open expression of frustrations in a way that validates everyone's worth and promotes mutual respect.
- **Invite Change through Careful Confrontation**: Instead of demanding changes in behavior, suggest them thoughtfully, focusing on specific observations rather than judgments. This approach should be inclusive, inviting discussion on possible solutions and alternatives and fostering a cooperative rather than confrontational atmosphere.
- **Cultivate Trust Proactively**: Building trust is essential, especially post-conflict. Leaders should approach conflict resolution with the expectation of mutual honesty and accountability, working to restore trust where it has eroded.
- **End the Blame Game**: Moving beyond blame is crucial to resolving conflicts effectively. Leaders should steer conversations away from fault-finding and towards constructive

solutions, asking forward-thinking questions about respectful next steps and future engagements.

- **Facilitate Unsticking**: Freeing team members from past grievances by focusing on the future allows for genuine change and prevents stagnation in personal grudges.
- **Champion Peacemaking**: Leaders should commit to being peacemakers, actively engaging in conflict resolution no matter the challenges, and valuing each team member's contributions while navigating through compromises.

By embedding these carefronting principles into their leadership practices, managers can alleviate generational tensions and unlock the full potential of their diverse teams.

CONCLUSIONS

Harnessing the strengths of a multigenerational workforce is essential for driving organizational success in today's dynamic business environment. The carefronting and ACORN business models are blueprints for leaders to effectively manage and integrate diverse generational talents, enhancing productivity and innovation. By accommodating employee differences, creating workplace choices, and operating from a theoretically sound management style, leaders can foster an inclusive culture that respects and utilizes the unique capabilities of each generation. Additionally, by nourishing retention and respecting employee competence and initiative, organizations can ensure that all team members are engaged and motivated, contributing positively to the company's goals.

Implementing these strategies requires a proactive and deliberate approach to leadership that recognizes generational differences and actively works to harness them. This involves creating an environment where open communication, mutual respect, and collaborative problem-solving are the norms. Through careful planning and implementation of these principles, leaders can transform potential intergenerational conflicts into opportunities for growth and collaboration, making the organization more resilient and adaptable to the changing business landscape. By prioritizing these approaches, companies can look forward to a future where the multigenerational workforce is not just a challenge to be managed but a significant asset to be leveraged.

> ## Box 15.1 Critical Take-Aways for Chapter 15
>
> 1 **Empower Gen X Leadership:** Position Generation X at the helm of multigenerational teams. Their broad understanding of older and younger generational values makes them ideal leaders to bridge gaps and enhance collaborative efforts across the workforce;
> 2 **Embrace ACORN Principles:** Implement the ACORN business model to create a workplace that is adaptable, inclusive, and responsive to the needs of all generations. Focus on accommodating differences, creating choices, and respecting employee competence to boost engagement and productivity;
> 3 **Foster a Culture of Carefronting:** Adopt carefronting strategies to address and mitigate conflicts constructively. This approach encourages open dialogue, mutual respect, and a cooperative atmosphere, turning potential conflicts into opportunities for team growth and cohesion.

NOTE

1 For research on applying the ACORN and Carefronting models to multiple generations at work see Kupperschmidt (2000, 2006).

REFERENCES

Augsburger, D. (1973). *She was caring enough to confront.* Regal Books.

Augsburger, D. (1981). *Caring enough to forgive.* Regal Books.

Kupperschmidt, B. (2000). Multigeneration employees: Strategies for effective management. *The Health Care Manager, 19*(1), 65–76. https://journals.lww.com/healthcaremanagerjournal/Citation/2000/19010/Multigeneration_Employees__Strategies_for.11.aspx

Kupperschmidt, B. (2006). Addressing multigenerational conflict: Mutual respect and carefronting as strategy. *OJIN: The Online Journal of Issues in Nursing, 11*(2). https://doi.org/10.3912/OJIN.Vol11No02Man03.

HOW TO IMPLEMENT MULTIGENERATION TRAINING

Abstract

This chapter underscores the critical role of training in enhancing effective intergenerational collaboration within modern organizations. As the workforce evolves with the inclusion of Generation Z, the need for structured training programs becomes more pronounced – not merely for skill enhancement but as a strategic imperative for organizational empowerment. Practical training serves dual purposes: it ensures all generational cohorts are adept with the latest technological tools, thereby maintaining a competitive market edge, and it fosters an ongoing learning environment crucial for building a resilient and adaptable workforce. Additionally, this training aligns multigenerational teams around shared goals and values, which is crucial for nurturing a cohesive corporate culture.

THE IMPERATIVE OF TRAINING IN TODAY'S ORGANIZATIONS

Training serves as a dual conduit in organizations. First, it ensures that employees across generations harness the latest technological tools and methodologies, essential for maintaining a competitive edge in digital-first markets. Second, it fosters an environment of continuous learning crucial for cultivating a resilient and adaptable workforce (Gerpott et al., 2021). Companies that invest robustly in comprehensive training programs report a 218% higher employee

DOI: 10.4324/9781032722696-19

income than companies without formalized training (American Society for Training and Development, 2024).

Moreover, the benefits of training extend beyond immediate productivity gains. Structured training programs are instrumental in shaping a cohesive corporate culture and aligning multigenerational teams around shared goals and values. In the context of Gen Z employees, who prioritize personal growth and meaningful work, training is not just a benefit but a necessity for engagement and retention (Morley et al., 2016).

Leaders are encouraged to view training as a strategic investment rather than a discretionary cost. Developing a curriculum that integrates soft skills, like communication and teamwork, with technical prowess adapts to diverse learning styles and generational expectations. Leveraging data-driven insights to tailor training initiatives that fill competency gaps and motivate and inspire a multigenerational workforce is advisable (Ochis, 2022).

CHECKLIST: HARNESSING DIVERSITY THROUGH MULTIGENERATIONAL TRAINING

✓ **Organize Comprehensive In-house Workshops**[1]:
  Craft an engaging two-day conference that delves into the complexities and opportunities of a multigenerational workforce. Begin with an introductory session on each generational cohort's distinct values and behaviors – Baby Boomers, Generation X, Millennials, and Generation Z. Address pressing issues like 'quiet quitting' and burnout, and examine the diverse perspectives of seasoned and novice employees. On the second day, focus on immersive multigenerational training, emphasizing leadership, communication, and conflict management through interactive role-plays and scenario-based activities to foster understanding and empathy among different age groups.

✓ **Launch Specialized Leadership Courses**:
  Implement targeted leadership training that equips current and future managers with the skills to appreciate and harness the unique characteristics of each generational group. This training should highlight how these traits influence engagement and

productivity and instruct leaders on managing a diverse workforce effectively. Emphasize process-oriented leadership strategies that provide the tools needed for diverse teams to collaborate and succeed.

✓ **Educate HR Managers on Generation Z**:

Prepare HR professionals for the future by tailoring training to better understand and meet Generation Z employees' expectations. Innovative approaches should be explored, such as gamifying the onboarding process and customizing job designs to appeal to younger workers. This preparation enables HR managers to craft roles and growth opportunities that resonate with the incoming workforce, fostering engagement from day 1.

✓ **Expand Executive Education**:

Encourage executive and middle-level managers to participate in optional seminars on effectively leading multigenerational teams. These sessions should provide actionable insights on optimizing team dynamics, aligning roles with generational strengths, and enhancing intergenerational collaboration. Specific learning points could include leveraging the process-oriented strengths of Baby Boomers, the cultural sensitivities of Generation Y, the technological savvy of Generation Z, and the versatile project management skills of Generation X.

By systematically implementing these strategies, organizations can bridge generational gaps and turn these differences into a strategic advantage, enhancing productivity and innovation across the board.

CONCLUSIONS

Training transcends its traditional boundaries, emerging as a strategic imperative to harness the full potential of a multigenerational workforce. Organizations that invest in comprehensive, tailored training programs enhance their competitive edge and foster a culture of continuous learning that is crucial for sustainability in rapidly evolving markets. Such programs cultivate a resilient and adaptable workforce by integrating soft and technical skills, adapting to varied learning styles, and addressing generational expectations.

Box 16.1 Key Take-Aways for Chapter 16

1   **Invest Strategically**: In training to transform it from a cost center into a vital tool for engagement and retention, particularly with Gen Z employees who seek meaningful work experiences;
2   **Harness Diversity**: Through comprehensive, tailored training programs that capitalize on each generational cohort's unique strengths and preferences, turning potential workplace challenges into opportunities for innovation and collaborative success;
3   **Adapt Training Methods**: To match varied learning styles and generational expectations, using data-driven insights to customize training that motivates and resonates with a multigenerational workforce.

NOTE

1   For a more extensive discussion on training tomorrow's leaders, see Ochis (2022).

REFERENCES

American Society for Training and Development. (2024). *Profiting from training! | Rewards from management training*. Business Training Experts. https://businesstrainingexperts.com/knowledge-center/training-roi/profiting-from-learning/

Gerpott, F. H., Lehmann-Willenbrock, N., Wenzel, R., & Voelpel, S. C. (2021). Age diversity and learning outcomes in organizational training groups: The role of knowledge sharing and psychological safety. *International Journal of Human Resource Management, 32*(18), 3777–3804. https://doi.org/10.1080/09585192.2019.1640763.

Morley, M. J., Slavic, A., Poór, J., & Berber, N. (2016). Training practices and organisational performance: A comparative analysis of domestic and international market oriented Organisations in Central & Eastern Europe. *Journal of East European Management Studies, 21*(4), 406–432. https://www.jstor.org/stable/44111958

Ochis, K. (2022, November 28). Managing the multigenerational workforce | AACSB. *The Association to Advance Collegiate Schools of Business (AACSB)*. https://www.aacsb.edu/insights/articles/2022/11/managing-the-multigenerational-workforce

HOW TO MANAGE TENSIONS BETWEEN GENERATIONS

Abstract

This chapter examines generational tensions and conflict management strategies in depth. It classifies tension types and provides solutions for managing conflicts effectively. It is a foundational guide for conflict prevention and implementing a conflict management system.

GENERATION CLASH: TYPES OF TENSIONS BETWEEN AGE GROUPS AT WORK

Tensions among Boomers and Millennials can primarily be categorized into three types: values-based, identity-based, and behavior-based[1] (Urick et al., 2017). Each tension type stems from each generation's worldview and work style:

- **Values-Based Tensions:** These tensions arise from differing core beliefs and values between generations. For instance, Baby Boomers often value loyalty and a strong work ethic, seeing long hours as a badge of honor. In contrast, Millennials might prioritize work-life balance and social responsibility, leading to potential clashes in work environment expectations.
- **Identity-Based Tensions**: These tensions are rooted in the generational identity and the stereotypes associated with each cohort. Such tensions often manifest as older generations perceiving younger ones as entitled or tech-obsessed, while younger generations might view their seniors as outdated or resistant to change. These perceptions can affect team dynamics and cooperation.

DOI: 10.4324/9781032722696-20

- **Behavior-Based Tensions**: These involve observable actions and habits that differ across generations, such as the adoption of technology or communication preferences. For example, Gen Z might prefer instant digital communication, whereas Boomers prefer more formal, face-to-face interactions.

Contextual factors also play a significant role in the emergence and intensity of these tensions. The work context – comprising work experience and workplace characteristics – and the broader societal context help shape how each generation views work and their roles within it. Leaders must understand these dynamics to design strategies that mitigate tension and promote a more inclusive work culture.

GENERATION CLASH: COPING MECHANISMS

Each generation brings its coping mechanisms and strategies to the table[2]:

- **Achievement-Oriented Strategies:** This approach bridges generational gaps through performance and communication adaptations. Individuals might adjust their communication style by altering the tone, medium, or language to better resonate with other generations. They emphasize common goals by highlighting results or achievements that appeal across age groups, fostering a sense of shared success and mutual respect.
- **Image-Oriented Strategies**: In this strategy, visibility and perception management are essential. Individuals ensure their efforts are conspicuous, often by maintaining a presence during traditional working hours or at critical meetings, thereby aligning with the work habits valued by older generations. They also strategically manage information to enhance their generational group's image, sharing successes and positive attributes that elevate their standing within the team.
- **Ego-Oriented Strategies**: The focus shifts to protecting personal interests and disengaging from conflict. Individuals employing this strategy prioritize their needs during interactions, ensuring their personal and professional requirements are

met. When tensions rise, they may withdraw or selectively ignore interactions that they perceive as unproductive or threatening to their well-being.

HOW TO MANAGE TENSIONS BETWEEN GENERATIONS: THE CONFLICT RESOLUTION MODEL

The Conflict Resolution Model provides a robust framework for addressing and resolving conflicts that preserves and strengthens intergenerational relationships. This model is rooted in the principles of integrative negotiation, which focuses on uncovering each party's natural interests and motivations, thereby fostering a cooperative rather than combative environment (Littlefield et al., 1993).

The essence of this approach lies in its view of conflict as a natural and essential aspect of organizational life. Rather than avoiding conflict, the model encourages leaders to embrace it as a catalyst for change and improvement, ensuring that all generational needs are considered and addressed. The process involves five key stages of problem-solving, detailed in Table 17.1, each designed to move from conflict identification to the collaborative development of solutions that satisfy all parties involved. This progression includes thoroughly assessing the underlying issues, brainstorming possible solutions, negotiating acceptable terms, and implementing agreed-upon actions.

By adopting this structured approach, leaders can transform potential generational clashes into productive dialogues that resolve immediate issues and build a foundation for ongoing positive interactions. This strategic embrace of conflict resolution ensures that organizations manage differences and actively leverage them to build a more dynamic, innovative, and resilient workforce.

ELEVATING CONFLICT MANAGEMENT: INTEGRATING STRATEGY WITH SYSTEMATIC APPROACHES

The transformation of conflict management from a reactive measure to a strategic element of organizational health marks a significant evolution in business practices (Lipsky et al., 2003). Implementing conflict management systems that are not just functional but strategic should interweave with broader organizational goals and policies.

Table 17.1 Stages of the Conflict Resolution Model

Stage	Description	Techniques
Problem orientation	Seeing problems as solvable showcases concern for both parties.	Explore interests cooperatively; show support towards the other party.
Defining and formulating the problem	Aspects are clearly classified, and goals are pinpointed; positions are acknowledged, and interests are explored.	Active listening; high-information exchange; grid formulation; interest prioritization.
Generation of alternative solutions	Based on brainstorming principles, ideas are combined, improved, and modified.	Deferment-of-judgment; quantity of ideas; variety of ideas about interests.
Decision-making	The best options are combined and developed into solutions that meet the critical interests of the parties.	Bridging solutions, expanding the pie, cost-cutting, compensation, and log rolling.
Solution identification and verification	A decision is made about the best solution; agreement is reached when all parties are satisfied and the main interests are met.	There is a return to areas of disagreement; a written contract may finalize the argument to ensure clearness.

Source: Adapted from Littlefield et al. (1993).

A well-architected conflict management system does more than resolve issues; it aligns with and enhances an organization's overall strategic framework, making conflict resolution a key driver of organizational efficiency and innovation.

The effectiveness of such systems hinges on several foundational elements:

1. A supportive organizational culture that fosters open communication and trust;
2. Unwavering commitment from top management to uphold;
3. Model conflict resolution principles; and
4. The presence of internal champions who advocate for and lead innovative resolution practices.

These systems are characterized by their comprehensive scope, cultural adaptiveness, accessibility, diverse resolution options, and robust support structures.[3] They are designed to transform conflicts from disruptive to productive, channeling them to reinforce and possibly innovate organizational practices (Lipsky et al., 2003).

Implementing such a system requires a nuanced approach that includes widespread training and an infrastructure that supports every level of the organization – from Generation Z newcomers to seasoned executives. By adopting this integrated approach, organizations can ensure that conflict management is not an isolated function but a fundamental aspect of their operational strategy, thereby enhancing their capacity to manage emergent tensions and deep-rooted conflicts, turning potential obstacles into opportunities for growth and development (Table 17.2).

CHECKLIST: MULTIGENERATIONAL CONFLICT MANAGEMENT SYSTEM

Table 17.2 Multigenerational Conflict Management System

Tier	Level	Description	Reasoning for Implementation
A prescribed organizational Conflict Resolution Model[4]	Organization level	The research findings indicate that multigenerational managers use a five-stage model based on problem orientation, problem definition and formulation, generation of alternative solutions, decision-making, and solution identification and verification.	Implementing a company-approved Conflict Resolution Model is essential for Generation Z to have a model for dealing with conflict.

(Continued)

Table 17.2 (Continued)

Encompassing Conflict Management System[5]	Systemic level	It incorporates the other tiers and is developed according to scope, culture, multiple access points, multiple options, and support structures.	Managers use disjointed strategies; there is a need for an encompassing preventive system.
Integration of generational differences	Organization level	Carefronting[6]; ACORN model.[7]	Communication to manage intergenerational tensions, unique characteristics, and preferences of generational groups is championed.
Intergenerational tensions management	Individual employees	Strategies are achievement, ego, and image-oriented to resolve values-based, identity-based, and behavior-based tensions.[8]	Individual employees learn to recognize intergenerational tensions and appropriately respond to them.
Principles of healthy relationships	Individual level of employees; Individual level of manager	The manager will clarify the group's area of freedom. Active listening, transparency, congruence, and I-messages.[9]	The model is similar to parent-child relationships, which is helpful in the context of transference. Managers should objectively observe the situation and decide upon management skills.

CONCLUSIONS

Mastering conflict management within multigenerational work-forces is essential for maintaining a dynamic and innovative organizational culture. The insights presented delineate a strategic framework for resolving generational tensions, using models like the Conflict Resolution Model by Littlefield et al. (1993), which outlines a structured approach to navigating disputes through integrative negotiation and collaborative problem-solving. This model emphasizes the significance of understanding all parties' real interests and motivations, transforming potential clashes into opportunities for synergy and organizational growth. By engaging in this model, organizations can ensure that conflicts are not merely resolved but are used as a springboard for fostering a culture of continuous improvement and adaptive change.

This chapter has dissected the nature of intergenerational conflicts and offered a strategic lens to view and resolve these tensions. Categorizing the types of conflicts – values-based, identity-based, and behavior-based – provides leaders with a clear understanding of the underlying issues that must be addressed.

Moreover, introducing a structured multigenerational conflict management system emphasizes a proactive approach to conflict management, advocating for recognizing and integrating generational differences into the broader organizational strategy.

Box 17.1 Critical Take-Aways for Chapter 17

1   **Embrace Integrative Negotiation:** Adopt conflict resolution strategies that focus on uncovering and aligning the underlying interests of all parties, fostering a cooperative environment;

2   **Implement Structured Models:** Utilize established models like the Conflict Resolution Model to provide a clear, step-by-step framework for managing disputes constructively;

3   **Identify Conflict Types:** To effectively tailor conflict resolution strategies, distinguish between values-based, identity-based, and behavior-based tensions.

NOTES

1   See Urick et al. (2017) for a discussion on workplace tensions between Boomers and Millennials.
2   See Urick et al. (2017) for a discussion on workplace tensions between Boomers and Millennials.
3   Lipsky et al. (2003) comprehensively describe conflict management systems.
4   See Littlefield et al. (1993) for further details on a conflict resolution model.
5   See Lipsky et al. (2003) on conflict management systems.
6   See Augsburger (1973) for the carefronting model.
7   See Kupperschmidt (2000) for integrating generational differences.
8   See Urick et al. (2017) for a comprehensive research on tensions between Boomers and Millenials.
9   See Gordon (1968, 2020) for the principles of healthy relationships.

REFERENCES

Augsburger, D. (1973). *She was caring enough to confront.* Regal Books.

Gordon, T. (1968). *A theory of parent effectiveness.* Harmony.

Gordon, T. (2020). *Origins of the Gordon model.* https://www.gordontraining. com/thomas-gordon/origins-of-the-gordon-model/

Kupperschmidt, B. (2000). Multigeneration employees: Strategies for effective management. *The Health Care Manager, 19*(1), 65–76. https://journals.lww. com/healthcaremanagerjournal/Citation/2000/19010/Multigeneration_ Employees__Strategies_for.11.aspx

Lipsky, D., Seeber, R., & Fincher, R. (2003). *Emerging systems for managing workplace conflict: Lessons from American corporations for managers and dispute resolution professionals.* Jossey-Bass.

Littlefield, L., Love, A., Peck, C., & Wertheim, E. (1993). A model for resolving conflict: Some theoretical, empirical and practical implications. *Australian Psychologist, 28*(2), 80–85. https://doi.org/10.1080/00050069308258880.

Urick, M., Hollensbe, E., Masterson, S., & Lyons, S. (2017). Understanding and managing intergenerational conflict: An examination of influences and strategies. In *Work, Aging and Retirement* (pp. 166–185). https://doi.org/ 10.1093/workar/waw009.

EIGHT ACTIONS YOU CAN TAKE TODAY

Abstract

This chapter presents a pragmatic eight-step framework for managing a multigenerational workforce. Designed for CEOs and senior leaders, this checklist offers immediate, actionable steps to enhance engagement, particularly among Gen Z employees, and address widespread disengagement. Each step is outlined with clear recommendations and cautions, ensuring effective implementation for immediate impact in the organization.

CULTIVATE MEANING THROUGH LOGOLEADERSHIP

Ensure Generation Z employees find purpose by integrating logotherapeutic techniques into leadership practices. By creating meaningful intergenerational collaborations, leaders can effectively disrupt disengagement and foster a commitment to professional standards and continuous improvement across all levels (Burger et al., 2008; Frankl, 1984) (Figure 18.1).

REVITALIZING ORGANIZATIONAL FRAMING TO FOSTER SYNERGY

Effective leadership in today's diverse workforce requires a nuanced approach to framing that elicits meaning and promotes engagement across generational divides. Framing allows leaders to establish shared understandings that shape behaviors and align them with

DOI: 10.4324/9781032722696-21

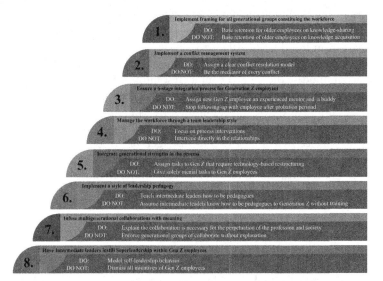

Figure 18.1 The Multigenerational Leadership Framework in Eight Actions.

Source: Figure by author.

organizational goals (Bean & Hamilton, 2006). This approach is critical in fostering employee commitment and facilitating adaptation to organizational changes to avoid sensemaking crises that deeply impact employees' identities and expectations. Specifically, the integration of younger employees often disrupts established norms, leading to tensions such as those observed between Boomers and Generation Z. The framework addresses these challenges by advocating for reframed interactions where knowledge-sharing is integral to retention and success, moving away from outdated models where Boomers might feel compelled to withhold information to secure their roles. This strategic reframing enhances cooperation and ensures that all generational groups contribute positively to the organization's dynamic environment.

OPTIMIZING CONFLICT MANAGEMENT THROUGH SYSTEMS

Effective conflict management in multigenerational settings involves a holistic approach that resolves disputes and fosters a culture of proactive engagement and mutual respect. A practical, comprehensive conflict management system ensures all levels of the organization – from frontline managers to Generation Z employees – access practical tools for addressing disagreements. This system is designed to accommodate the diverse conflict resolution needs across different age groups, enhancing intergenerational cooperation and maintaining healthy workplace relationships. It supports Generation Z employees by providing them with structured guidance on navigating workplace dynamics and aids managers in fostering a cohesive team environment. This approach mitigates conflict and strengthens the organizational fabric by embedding conflict resolution capabilities at every level of interaction within the company.

STREAMLINING GENERATION Z INTEGRATION: A TACTICAL APPROACH

The integration of Generation Z starts with pre-onboarding, where accurate job descriptions help candidates gauge job fit, minimizing early job disillusionment risks (Dharmasiri et al., 2014). The onboarding process introduces them to company culture and expectations, supported by mentorship and peer connections to ease their socialization (Klinghoffer et al., 2019). During the probation period, new hires handle empowering tasks with the option to shape their career paths actively. Post-probation, the focus shifts to more in-depth training and responsibilities, ensuring alignment with seasoned employees' rewards and fostering equity and professional growth. Evaluations throughout the integration mix formal and informal check-ins, adjusting roles and workloads to maintain engagement and support development. This strategy prepares Generation Z for substantive roles and aligns their professional growth with organizational goals.

IMPLEMENT LEADERSHIP PEDAGOGY

Adopt a critical pedagogy approach to prepare all employees to act as agents of change within the organization. This involves transforming experienced employees into adept pedagogues who can effectively pass on professional knowledge and skills to Generation Z employees, enhancing their readiness to innovate and adapt.

PROMOTE SUPERLEADERSHIP AND SELF-LEADERSHIP

Encourage employees at all levels to lead themselves and others. This dual approach empowers experienced employees and helps Generation Z employees develop Self-leadership skills essential for effectively organizing and managing their responsibilities (Manz & Sims, 1991).

ENHANCE TEAM LEADERSHIP AND ADRESS COHESION

Focus on process-oriented leadership to ensure effective team dynamics and integration of generational differences. Monitoring and diagnosing team interactions helps achieve desired outcomes while respecting and leveraging the unique contributions of each generational group (Hill, 2016; Kupperschmidt, 2000). By understanding and addressing specific generational characteristics, leaders can foster a cohesive work environment that leverages diverse perspectives and strengths (Kupperschmidt, 2000).

FOSTER AN ENVIRONMENT OF CONTINUOUS IMPROVEMENT AND COLLABORATION

Encourage a culture where feedback and development are continuous, allowing Generation Z and other generational cohorts to feel valued and understood. This culture promotes not only personal growth but also organizational adaptability and resilience.

By implementing these strategies, leaders can create a dynamic and inclusive workplace that addresses the challenges a multigenerational workforce poses and harnesses all employees' diverse strengths and perspectives, leading to enhanced innovation, productivity, and engagement.

MULTILAYERED LEADERSHIP

In the multigenerational workforce, the role of intermediate leaders is crucial in translating top-level strategies into daily operational realities that directly affect Generation Z's engagement and integration within the company. These intermediary leaders, often equivalent to middle managers, act as the vital link between the overarching organizational objectives and the individual experiences of younger employees, implementing meso strategies that shape everyday workplace interactions and dynamics. Intermediate leaders ensure that the engagement tactics are theoretically sound and pragmatically practical by focusing on specific leadership approaches. This involves adapting communication styles, mentoring approaches and conflict resolution techniques that resonate with Generation Z, reducing disengagement, and enhancing their contribution to the organization's goals. This strategic alignment across different leadership levels guarantees that the entire spectrum of the workforce is engaged, productive, and harmoniously integrated.

CONCLUSIONS

In today's multifaceted corporate environment, the capacity to navigate Multigenerational Leadership is not merely beneficial – it is critical for fostering a vibrant and effective workplace. This framework emphasizes the necessity of deploying specialized strategies tailored to both upper and middle management tiers to fully engage Generation Z. These methods, which span from comprehensive pre-onboarding initiatives to sophisticated conflict management tactics, are designed to ensure that every employee, particularly those from Generation Z, is recognized, appreciated, and seamlessly integrated into the corporate fabric.

To implement these insights, begin immediately in your next operational cycle. Methodically introduce each strategy, mindful of the specific actions to embrace and pitfalls to avoid. By methodically applying these eight transformative actions, you are actively contributing to crafting an environment that transcends mere diversity. This approach enriches your organizational culture and solidifies a genuinely inclusive and collaborative workplace, setting a new standard for business operations.

Box 18.1 Key Take-Aways for Chapter 18

1 **Strategize Proactively**: Deploy customized engagement strategies tailored for all levels of management to connect with Generation Z effectively;

2   **Manage Conflicts Intelligently:** Implement refined conflict management frameworks to nurture a culture of respect and mutual understanding across generations;
3   **Empower through Leadership:** Utilize dynamic leadership models that encourage self-leadership and foster robust mentorship relationships within the workforce.

REFERENCES

Bean, C. J., & Hamilton, F. E. (2006). Leader framing and follower sensemaking: Response to downsizing in the brave new workplace. *Human Relations, 59*(3), 321–349. https://doi.org/10.1177/0018726706064177.

Burger, D. H., Crous, F., & Roodt, G. (2008). Logo-OD: The applicability of logotherapy as an OD intervention. *South African Journal of Industrial Psychology, 34*(1), 32–41. https://doi.org/10.4102/sajip.v34i3.388.

Dharmasiri, A., Buckley, M., Baur, J., & Sahatjian, Z. (2014). A historical approach to realistic job previews. *Journal of Management History, 20*, 10 1108-06-2012–0046.

Frankl, V. E. (1984). *Man's search for meaning.* Square Press.

Hill, S. (2016). *Team leadership* (P. Northouse, Ed.; Leadership (7th)). Sage Publications.

Klinghoffer, D., Young, C., & Haspas, D. (2019). Every new employee needs an onboarding buddy. *Harvard Business Review.* https://hbr.org/2019/06/every-new-employee-needs-an-onboarding-buddy

Kupperschmidt, B. (2000). Multigeneration employees: Strategies for effective management. *The Health Care Manager, 19*(1), 65–76. https://journals.lww.com/healthcaremanagerjournal/Citation/2000/19010/Multigeneration_Employees__Strategies_for.11.aspx

Manz, C., & Sims, H. (1991). SuperLeadership: Beyond the myth of heroic leadership. *Organizational Dynamics, 19*(4), 18–35. https://doi.org/10.1016/0090-2616(91)90051-A.

BONUS CHAPTER: REDEFINING LEADERSHIP FOR A NEW AI ERA

Abstract

The challenge for leaders is not just about managing a team but about leveraging cutting-edge technologies like artificial intelligence (AI) to enhance the capabilities of a multigenerational workforce. This bonus chapter presents a meticulously crafted checklist designed to guide leaders through the strategic integration of AI within their organizations. Tailored to accommodate the unique dynamics and varied skill sets of different generational cohorts, the checklist offers practical, actionable steps.

As artificial intelligence (AI) technology advances and integrates into workplace dynamics, a critical challenge for today's leaders is managing a multigenerational workforce and steering these diverse teams through the complexities introduced by AI. The convergence of generational insights and AI capabilities has given rise to new leadership strategies essential for any forward-thinking organization (Anderson & Raine, 2023).

EMBRACING AI IN MULTIGENERATIONAL LEADERSHIP

In an era where digital natives and seasoned professionals coexist, the infusion of AI into daily operations can bridge the technological gap between generations. AI tools offer personalized learning experiences, predictive analytics for enhanced decision-making, and automation of routine tasks, thereby freeing up employees for complex

DOI: 10.4324/9781032722696-22

problem-solving and innovation. Leaders are tasked with integrating AI in ways that complement the strengths of each generation, fostering an environment where both human expertise and machine efficiency thrive.

TRANSFORMATIVE LEADERSHIP WITH AI

Leadership in the AI era demands adaptability, vision, and a continuous learning mindset. It involves understanding the implications of AI from a technological standpoint and its impact on organizational culture and employee engagement. This requires leaders to proactively upskill themselves and their teams to work alongside AI effectively. By doing so, they harness the collaborative power of human-AI interaction to solve problems more creatively and enhance productivity.[1]

CULTIVATING TRUST AND TRANSPARENCY

One of the fundamental challenges in adopting AI is building trust among employees across generational divides. Transparency about how AI is used, its benefits, and its limitations is crucial. Leaders must ensure that AI implementations are ethical and that decisions made by AI are fair and transparent.[2] This builds employee confidence, ensuring that AI is seen as an enabler of success rather than a threat to job security.

LEVERAGING AI FOR CUSTOMIZED EMPLOYEE EXPERIENCE

AI's real-time ability to analyze vast amounts of data allows leaders to deliver a more customized employee experience. From tailored training programs that match individual learning paces and styles to personalized career development plans, AI can significantly enhance how organizations support their employees' professional growth, especially in diverse generational settings (Ochis, 2023b).

STRATEGIC DECISION-MAKING ENHANCED BY AI

Finally, AI dramatically enhances leaders' ability to make data-driven decisions. AI can guide strategic decisions informed by a deep understanding of external market conditions and internal workforce dynamics by providing insights into market trends, employee performance, and operational efficiencies. Leaders who integrate AI insights into their strategic planning can better anticipate changes and adapt strategies aligning with organizational goals and employee expectations (Ochis, 2023a).

Box 19.1 Leading Across Ages: The AI Integration Playbook

- Evaluate and Identify AI Opportunities:
  Conduct a thorough assessment of your current processes and identify areas where AI can add significant value. Focus on tasks that can be automated to free up employee time for more strategic activities, such as customer engagement and innovation. Utilize AI to enhance decision-making through data-driven insights and analytics.
- Develop a Tailored AI Training Program:
  Create training modules tailored to different generational needs and learning styles. For younger employees, leverage interactive and tech-driven training methods. Consider more structured, step-by-step training sessions for older generations demonstrating AI's value and practical utility in their daily tasks.
- Foster an AI-positive culture:
  Cultivate an organizational culture that views AI as an ally rather than a threat. Highlight success stories where AI has augmented team capabilities, not replaced them. Encourage open dialogues about AI's role and impact, addressing concerns and showcasing how AI implementation has led to job enhancement, not elimination.
- Implement AI Ethics Guidelines:
  Establish clear guidelines on the ethical use of AI within your organization. Ensure all AI applications comply with industry standards and respect privacy and data integrity. This will build trust among employees across all ages and position your company as a leader in responsible AI usage.
- Measure and Adapt AI Strategies:
  Measure the outcomes and impacts of AI integrations regularly. Use these insights to adapt and refine AI strategies, ensuring they align with corporate goals and employee well-being. Engage with

employees from various generations to get feedback on AI tools and strategies, adjusting to better meet their needs and enhance their work experience.

- Reskills or Hire recruits with AI studies[3]:

As the business sector continues to increase its reliance on AI, more business schools are determining how to incorporate the technology into their classrooms. About 74% of business schools currently are teaching generative AI (*Graduate Business Curriculum Roundtable*, 2023).

By following this checklist, leaders can harness the full potential of AI to foster a more productive, engaged, and harmonious multigenerational workplace.

CONCLUSIONS

Integrating AI into leadership practices is not just about technological adoption but about transforming leadership to be more inclusive, insightful, and innovative. As AI reshapes industries, leaders must redefine their roles, embracing AI as a pivotal element in their strategic toolkit for managing today's diverse and multigenerational teams.

Box 19.2 Key Take-Aways for Chapter 19

1. **Upgrade Leadership Skills**: Adapt leadership styles incorporating AI, focusing on continuous learning and adaptability to drive innovation;

2. **Personalize Employee Growth**: Utilize AI's analytical power to customize learning and development, aligning with individual career aspirations across generations;

3. **Enhance Strategic Decisions**: Leverage AI-driven insights for superior decision-making, ensuring organizational agility and strategic foresight in rapidly changing markets.

NOTES

1 See Ochis (2023) *Become a Strategic AI Leader: How AI is Game-Changing for Leaders* for a further discussion on the nexus between AI and leadership and learn four strategies to implement AI as a leader.
2 For a discussion on ethical considerations about AI, see Ochis (2023).
3 See Ochis (2024) *Navigating the AI Revolution* to explore the multiple ways AI in taught in business schools.

REFERENCES

Anderson, J., & Raine, L. (2023, June 21). *As AI spreads, experts predict the best and worst changes in digital life by 2035.* Pew Research Center: Internet, Science & Tech. https://www.pewresearch.org/internet/2023/06/21/as-ai-spreads-experts-predict-the-best-and-worst-changes-in-digital-life-by-2035/

Graduate Business Curriculum Roundtable. (2023). https://gbcroundtable.org/GenAI

Ochis, K. (2023a, December 28). AI organizational revolutions to watch out for in 2024: Navigating the transformative winds of organizational change. *Forbes.* https://www.forbes.com/sites/forbescoachescouncil/2023/12/28/become-a-strategic-ai-leader-how-ai-is-game-changing-for-leaders/

Ochis, K. (2023b, December 28). Become a strategic AI leader: How AI is game-changing for leaders. Forbes. https://www.forbes.com/sites/forbescoachescouncil/2023/12/28/become-a-strategic-ai-leader-how-ai-is-game-changing-for-leaders/

Ochis, K. (2024, February 5). Navigating the AI revolution. *The Association to Advance Collegiate Schools of Business (AACSB).* https://www.aacsb.edu/insights/articles/2024/02/navigating-the-ai-revolution

CONCLUSION

Abstract

This chapter concludes the pivotal exploration into the dynamics of Generation Z within the modern workforce, underscoring a transformative shift in today's corporate landscape. With Generation Z entering the workforce, traditional engagement models are increasingly challenged, necessitating a reevaluation of management strategies to prevent disengagement and turnover. This narrative delves into the distinct attributes of Generation Z, highlighting their digital fluency, preference for flexible work arrangements, and unique communication styles. It argues for a proactive, strategic approach to Multigenerational Leadership that accommodates the nuanced demands of this new cohort while fostering an inclusive environment for all generations. This chapter provides actionable insights and tools for business leaders to enhance engagement, optimize intergenerational collaboration, and leverage the diverse strengths of their workforce, thereby driving organizational success in a rapidly evolving business environment.

CONCLUSIONS

In conclusion, the entry of Generation Z into the workforce has sparked a transformative shift in organizational dynamics, compelling leaders to reconsider traditional engagement strategies and adapt

DOI: 10.4324/9781032722696-23

to the evolving landscape of a multigenerational workforce. As outlined in *Gen Z in Work*, this newest cohort presents not only challenges but also significant opportunities for innovation and productivity. Their distinct characteristics – digital fluency, unique communication preferences, and a hunger for meaningful engagement – demand a nuanced leadership approach that goes beyond conventional practices.

For leaders to not just survive but thrive in this new era, it is crucial to adopt strategies that not only address the distinctive needs of Generation Z but also harmonize the diverse expectations of all generational cohorts. By fostering an environment that values inclusivity, collaboration, and empowerment, organizations can enhance engagement across all age groups, thereby mitigating the risks associated with disengagement and turnover. This emphasis on unity and teamwork is key to success in the evolving workforce.

The time to act is now. The costs of inaction – alienated employees, lost productivity, and eroded competitive advantage – are too great. Leaders must swiftly implement adaptive strategies that are attuned to the complexities of today's workforce. This involves embracing technological advancements, leveraging the strengths of each generational group, and building a culture conducive to open communication and continuous learning. The urgency of this call to action is a testament to the rapid changes in the workforce and the need for immediate response and adaptation.

Gen Z in Work is not just a resource but a crucial one. It equips leaders with actionable insights and practical tools to navigate this transformation successfully. It advocates for a leadership paradigm that is proactive, responsive, and rooted in a profound understanding of the psychosocial dynamics that shape workplace behavior. As organizations teeter on the edge of this generational threshold, the ability to engage a diverse workforce will be a defining factor in their lasting success and legacy.

This book is not just a guide but a call to action for all business leaders to reshape their strategies and lead with an inclusive and forward-thinking vision. The future of work is here, and it is rich with potential for those who dare to lead it.

Box 20.1 Key Take-Aways for Chapter 20

1   **Embrace Digital Integration:** Harness Generation Z's tech-savviness to drive innovation and efficiency in your workplace. Their digital fluency can be a significant asset in an increasingly technology-driven world;

2   **Foster Inclusive Cultures:** Develop a workplace culture that celebrates diversity and inclusion across all generational cohorts. Recognizing and valuing diverse perspectives can enhance creativity and problem-solving within teams;

3   **Customize Engagement Strategies:** Tailor engagement strategies to meet the unique needs and expectations of Generation Z. Personalized approaches resonate more effectively with this cohort, leading to higher job satisfaction and retention rates;

4   **Promote Flexibility and Autonomy:** Offer flexible working conditions and greater autonomy over work. This aligns with Generation Z's expectations and encourages a sense of ownership and responsibility;

5   **Invest in Continuous Learning:** Commit to ongoing professional development opportunities to cater to Generation Z's appetite for growth and learning. This investment can also help keep the workforce's skills current and relevant;

6   **Enhance Communication:** Optimize communication styles to meet the preferences of a multigenerational workforce. Transparent and frequent communication helps build trust and align goals across different age groups;

7   **Strengthen Leadership Development:** Equip your leaders with the skills necessary to manage a diverse workforce effectively. Effective leadership is pivotal in bridging generational divides and fostering an environment of mutual respect and collaboration;

8   **Address 'Quiet Quitting':** Address the issue of 'quiet quitting' head-on by identifying its root causes and implementing strategies to engage disenchanted employees actively. This proactive approach can significantly reduce turnover and improve organizational morale;

9   **Implement Collaborative Technologies:** Leverage collaborative tools that facilitate seamless interaction and teamwork across different locations and time zones. This is particularly crucial for engaging remote or hybrid employees, including those from Generation Z;

10 **Evaluate Impact Regularly**: Regularly assess the effectiveness of your engagement and management strategies to ensure they remain responsive to the evolving needs of your workforce. Continuous evaluation and adaptation are crucial to staying relevant and effective in a dynamic corporate landscape.

Each of these take-aways encourages leaders to be proactive and responsive, ensuring that strategies reflect the unique attributes of Generation Z and enhance the overall cohesion and productivity of a diverse workforce.

INDEX

Printed in the United States
by Baker & Taylor Publisher Services